GLAMOUR
IN FASHION

GLAMOUR
IN FASHION

David Bond

GUINNESS PUBLISHING

Editor: Paola Simoneschi
Picture Editor: P. Alexander Goldberg
Design and Layout: Barry Lowenhoff

© David Bond 1992

Published in Great Britain by Guinness Publishing Ltd,
33 London Road, Enfield, Middlesex

Typeset in Walbaum Roman
by Ace Filmsetting Ltd, Frome, Somerset
Printed and bound in Italy by New Interlitho SpA,
Milan

'Guinness' is a registered trademark of Guinness Publishing Ltd

A catalogue record for this book is available from the
British Library

ISBN 0–85112–516–6

Contents

Preface

There are many interpretations of glamour. It means different things to different people. For some, it can be as blatant as a bare-breasted 'Page Three' girl, or a male pop star in over-tight leather jeans, while for others it can mean status-conscious and impressive – the perfectly groomed, 'no expense spared' couture-dressed woman and the bespoke-tailored business tycoon.

The most popular and persistent image of glamour in fashion must surely be that of the movie-star goddess in her body-clinging evening gown – Marlene Dietrich, Rita Hayworth and Marilyn Monroe are three names that immediately spring to mind.

A combination of good looks, lithe physique and excellence in sport can also project an aura of glamour, as can the military hero in immaculate uniform.

On the other hand, glamour can be simple and uncontrived – glowing good health, a charming manner and a memorable smile.

Section One
Glamour's Golden Age

Despite the unsettling effects of the First World War, the 1920s stand out as a bright, youth-orientated period with great enthusiasm for its own time. Nostalgia for the recent past, so popular in later decades, held

The Late 20s

little appeal for the post-war generation after the horrors of the conflict. People had confidence in the future, and expressions of 'new beginnings', 'new age' and 'brave new world', which were to become such clichés in later years, were genuinely heartfelt when they were first used.

Opposite: Stylish clothes and 'good time' living were enjoyed by the affluent post-war generation.

Innovation characterised the times. Young men and women in their 20s and 30s set the style of the decade and London, Paris, Berlin and New York were exciting centres of new ideas. They all had a rich share of creative personalities — writers, musical and theatrical talents, photographers, architects, interior decorators and fashion designers. America's influence, which was to be such a strong force during the century, had already arrived and American culture was admired and widely followed. Popular music and films in particular, were new forms of mass communication that appealed to all nationalities and classes. Even the aristocratic Europeans realised they no longer had a monopoly on social trends and acknowledged the new transatlantic influences. England's Prince of Wales, his set and London society's notorious 'bright young things' were known to enjoy watching the latest films, admiring the film stars' looks and dancing to American hit records. The jazz musician with his haunting saxophone was the new Pied Piper and, for those who had the time, money and inclination, social life was rather like a continual New Year's Eve party.

Cole Porter's famous song 'Anything Goes', although written for the well-known early-30s musical of the same name, aptly captured the frivolity of the fun-loving 20s with its endearing, light-hearted mood that was never quite repeated in any of the following decades. When Porter wrote 'In olden days a glimpse of stocking was looked on as something shocking. Now, heaven knows, anything goes', he must have been thinking of the impact of the knee-length hemlines of the simple chemise dresses of 1926 compared to the floor-sweeping dresses worn when he was a boy at the beginning of the century. The whole ideal of what constituted an attractive, fashionably-dressed woman had been revolutionised in less than 15 years. Fashion plates of 1912 and 1926 look as if they illustrate decorative dress worn by two totally different cultures. In many ways, they do.

The beginning of a fundamental breakaway from the long-established concept of fashion changes within the confines of long, elaborately-dressed hair, ornate hats and the liberal use of decorated fabrics covering up a firmly-corsetted figure, had already started just before the First World War.

Technological and political developments were quickening the pace of social change and many of the younger generation, with their increasingly active lives, were ready to welcome more practical attitudes towards fashion.

The creative talents of advanced designers, particularly Paul Poiret and — a little later — Coco Chanel, seemed to sense intuitively the need for change, and pioneered major alternations in the way women looked. Although their styles differed, they shared a similar, basic original concept. All the new fashions were based on a less restricted, lithe, youthful body; clothes were designed in lighter, softer, more fluid fabrics; high-boned collars, stiff fabrics pulled tightly into unnaturally small waists and long, complicated skirts were replaced by open-necked, lightly-shaped bodices, unemphasised waists and much more slender skirts that daringly revealed the ankles.

The First World War accelerated even greater changes in society which, in turn, were reflected in still more liberated styles of dress. Post-war fashion ignored the natural curves of the female figure — they were considered a disadvantage. Breasts were flattened, waists bypassed and bodices fell loosely from the shoulders to barely-indicated, hip-level waistlines. The dominant hat shape became the pull-on, helmet-shaped cloche. Hairstyles were cut ever shorter, culminating in the severely mannish 'Eton crop', and skirt lengths inched progressively upwards to the kneecap, making well-shaped legs a woman's most prized asset. By the mid-20s, the fashion revolution was complete. The young loved the fast-moving and dramatic changes; they revelled in their shock value. Not surprisingly, many older people condemned the new fashion ideals as ugly and

For many men, the sight of young
women showing silk-stockinged
knees and thighs represented
glamour-dressing in its most potent
form.

Far right: Simple wrap-around coats with fur trimmings and cloche hats were popular fashion choices in the late 20s.

Right: By 1927, the evening-dress line had softened with uneven hems and dipping panels.

felt that they had abandoned the traditional qualities of charm, prettiness and femininity.

Fashionable women's clothes had reached such an unprecedented degree of simplicity and uniformity it seems they could go no further in the evolution of modern dress. The basic silhouette consisted of a straight, knee-length tunic or chemise shape, often collarless and, for the evening and the summer, frequently sleeveless. Dressmaking had never been so easy and it would be another 40 years before the skimpy lines of the 20s were surpassed by the thigh-high mini-shift dresses of the 60s.

Once the daring of 1920s fashion at its most minimal had been accepted, become mainstream and then common-place, designers realised the need for fashion to develop in some other less obvious and more sophisticated way. After the revolution there was scope for some form of counter-revolution. Glamour was about to make its early appearances and add a much needed new dimension to the way style-conscious women looked.

Women's magazines for autumn 1927 all reported a changing mood. There was much talk of revived femininity and increased elegance. *Vogue* for September, in its 'Paris Forecasts', noted: 'A less stereotyped mode permits greater individuality of dress than the uniform fashions of past seasons.' It was the beginning of the first new fashion direction of the decade, an appealing change, an overall 'femininising' of the way women looked to something more alluring and sexy, without losing the easy-to-wear lines of unrestricted fit and the flowing silhouette.

The stylish image became more sophisticated and, although still self-consciously 'modern', it was slightly older and more worldly than the popular idea of the decade's hyperactive, flighty flappers; a more languid, blasé pose was often cultivated.

Obvious make-up – which was no longer a novelty – was more skilfully applied; face powder carefully dusted on;

eyes outlined; lids shaded and eyebrows finely plucked or shaved-off altogether. Brow lines were clearly drawn on at a higher-than-normal level, with an arched line giving the characteristically slightly surprised, quizzical look to fash-ionably made-up faces. Cheeks were always rouged and lips were painted very red, with an almost varnished appearance, and outlined into a rather pert shape, often called the 'cupid's bow', 'rosebud' or, more extremely, 'divine bee-stung lips'.

Along with blatantly painted faces, the 'neat little head' was very much a part of the 20s image. About 1927, the severely-short styles began to soften with gentle, flirty, waved fronts and sides, and women started to grow their hair longer to give scope for more feminine styles. It was a rather tentative trend at first. However, by the end of the decade many fashion-conscious women considered the boyish 'Eton

Far left: Louise Brooks displaying two of glamour's golden age's classic looks — the short, sleek bob and the one-shouldered lame sheath dress.

Left: Greta Garbo's haunting beauty and romantic European image made her one of the most memorable stars in the history of the cinema.

crop' and 'shingle' passé and had grown their hair long enough to pin into sophisticated-looking rolls and chignons, or have it arranged in rather stylised waves or curls on the nape of the neck. Blonde hair was becoming very fashionable, together with suntanned faces. Edwardian women would have been appalled at the idea of unashamedly-dyed blonde hair and sunburnt skin, but to the more hard-edged beauty ideals of the late 20s, it was a newly-admired cosmetic 'fix'. Anita Loos's highly successful book, *Gentlemen Prefer Blondes*, had done much to popularise the idea that blondes really *did* have more fun.

Although there was greater variety in hairstyles by the turn of the decade, immaculate grooming was considered all-important. Hair was usually neatly parted in the centre or at the side and brushed to a sheen but, if the right degree of natural gloss was felt to be lacking, it was helped to look fashionably sleek with brilliantine oil.

Hats, like hairstyles, were softer and more flattering, and although shallow-looking berets and draped skullcaps were the newest trends, most styles until 1930 continued to be based on the deep, head-fitting cloche. Details of shape, however, were far more varied. Crowns were arranged in

Softer versions of the helmet-shaped cloche gained favour in 1928 and '29.

folds, sometimes like a draped turban, or the outline was softened with swathed silk or veiling. Brims turned back to show more of the face and hairline, other styles dipped flatteringly at the front or over one eye, or curved out at the sides. Summer picture hats had large, wavy brims. Jewelled clips, pins or buckles were often added as a decoration. Hats were a great talking point – a simple, slender-line dress, suit or coat topped with a dashing hat in shiny straw, velvet or satin as the focus of an outfit often proved to be stunningly effective for making an entrance at a fashionable restaurant. It became a popular new format for smart dressing and,

although the designs changed continually, it remained so during the following two decades.

Female curves, which had been considered undesirable and ignored by high fashion for so long, were at least no longer deliberately suppressed in the revised silhouette of the late 20s. Fit moved a little closer to the body and the outline of the breasts and waist were gently shadowed. Waistline details were still low but they were gradually moving nearer to their natural place. Hips were definitely more fitted and became the focal point of many designs. Skirts flared from the thighs and fluted out to rather

uncertain hemlines. There were predictions of longer skirts, but the impression of increased length was achieved first by the general elongation of the silhouette with its higher waists and subtle shaping, rather than a definite all-round drop in skirt lengths. Uneven hemlines, deeper panels and skirts that dipped noticeably at the back paved the way for longer skirts and gave a less skimpy, more flowing line, but still managed to look young.

To complement the growing trend for femininity, 'soft touches' became a characteristic feature of the new fashions. Sensual fabrics like velvet, satin, crêpe de chine, tulle and georgette were widely used and perfect for the design details of the time. Necklines were softly tied, draped into scarf collars, arranged as cowls or trimmed with jabots. Sleeves either fanned out at the wrists or the fullness was delicately caught into long cuffs buttoned into tiny loops. Dress bodices were often designed to wrap over and fasten on a lightly-swathed hipline with a bow or a jewel-clipped sash.

Sinuous fabric and design combined brilliantly in evening dresses. Gold satin was draped over beige chiffon, oyster-coloured, metallic brocade with finely pleated crêpe de chine, and silky, black panné velvet was used for long-torsoed dresses, teamed with layers of gold-flecked black net in handkerchief-pointed skirts. Alternatively, black velvet was designed in simple, sleeveless dresses with crossover bodices and softly-folding, long side-panels, lined in white satin.

Furs were rarely thought of as crass in the early decades of the 20th century. They were an established part of fashion and their use in the late 20s, combined with soft, fluid dress fabrics, added another dimension to the 'touch appeal', allure and emerging glamour in dressing.

Fox furs, in particular, were often used as an accessory with dresses and suits, draped casually over the shoulder or arms. They were also used effectively as part of a jacket or coat to give a softer outline to the silhouette. Collars, cuffs, front edgings and hems were trimmed with fur, sometimes all on the same garment. Evening wraps in gold and white brocade, or silver and white lamé, extravagantly collared and cuffed in white fox, wrapped and held on one hip, forming a shimmering cocoon-shape over a flimsy white satin or chiffon dress, with a fluttering uneven hemline showing below the wrap, presented one of the most appealing images of early glamour ideals.

Coco Chanel was arguably the greatest dress designer of the 20th century. Her enduring influence on fashion is nothing less than phenomenal. She was a known designer as early as the 1910s and today, many years after her death, Karl Lagerfeld cleverly interprets and adapts her style for the Chanel label and to the fashion tastes of the 1990s, making the Chanel image, with all the spin-offs in ready-to-wear clothes, fragrances and accessories, better known and more commercially available than ever before.

In the late 20s, Chanel was at the height of her first period as a major influence on fashion. Her concept of the new youthful glamour had done much to replace traditional ways of showing rank and status through richness of dress.

She believed in understatement and was one of the first designers to promote the idea that 'less was more' when it came to chic and stylishness. Chanel designs were deceptively simple and very edited for the time. She pared away the excess of trimmings, decorations and contrived shapes and rejected obviously rich and gaudy fabrics in favour of high quality but more plain, lightweight tweeds, fine wool crêpe, subtle jersey and soft-handling silks, often in neutral colours like black, navy, creamy beige and pearl grey. She paid great attention to cut and fit — her clothes were skilfully shaped to flatter the figure without restricting it. Shoulders, sleeves, waists and hips all allowed for ease of movement but never looked over-loose or baggy. They had a young, fresh, effortless, yet immaculate quality which made women look expensively dressed in a much more subtle way.

Chanel, with her slim, dark, Gallic looks was the best advertisement for her clothes. She mixed with many of the rich and famous international set of the period and was regularly photographed looking enviably chic in one of her own designs.

Over 60 years ago, Chanel introduced glamour ideas in fashion that have become perennial favourites: suits in fine wool and tweed with toning silk revers and blouses; cardigan jackets edged with clever, pseudo-military braid; simple top coats lined with expensive fur; blazer jackets in sequins worn over flimsy, chiffon evening dresses and, most successful of all, 'the little black dress'. This was the term used for slip-like black dresses with minimal design details in fine wool, silk or velvet, used as a background or foil for showing off jewellery. The black velvet sheath dress, worn with pearl earrings and a matching necklace, became one of the glamour classics of the century.

Until the 20s, wearing fake jewellery, particularly in any great quantity, would have been considered very bad taste indeed. Chanel was not against real jewels; in fact, she had an impressive collection of her own, but she also liked the idea of less expensive, 'false' jewellery, worn for its own design value and specially styled to suit a particular transitory fashion trend. She popularised costume jewellery as a part of the overall fashion picture.

Apart from her well-known pearls-with-almost-every-thing dictum, Chanel also successfully promoted stud earrings, jewelled hats and lapel pins and, very characteristic of the time, bracelets. High-arm 'slave bracelets' were worn with sleeveless dresses and for added sleeve interest on ultra-simple dresses; graduated in rows at the wrists, several diamanté bracelets worn over both sleeve ends of a black jersey dress, or on top of long black suede gloves, gave a very sophisticated femme fatale look to many city outfits.

Although the now legendary 'Chanel look' has made her the best-remembered name of the 20s, there were several other talented designers who were also part of the trendsetting elite of the period and probably considered of equal importance at the time.

Paris-based Irishman, Edward Molyneux, was greatly admired for the flattering, quiet perfection of his designs. They were never 'strong designer statements' but always struck just the right fashion note and were slow to date. Women loved wearing his clothes, which included spotted silk pyjamas, and the low-back, clinging, white satin evening dress that he designed for a suntanned Gertrude Lawrence to wear in the famous balcony scene in Noel Coward's *Private Lives* made a stunning and lasting impression.

Jean Patou was another important designer who promoted more feminine, flowing lines. After the dipping hemlines of 1927 and 1928, he dropped the hemline decisively in his autumn 1929 collection to mid-calf for day clothes and ankle- or floor-length for evening dresses, setting the seal on the much longer lengths of the early 30s.

Madeleine Vionnet was very much a designer's de-signer. Her clothes were beautifully made, superbly cut, intricate, individual designs that were to become collectors' pieces. Unlike Chanel, her style was difficult to commercial-ise. She was well-respected by the fashion world and is probably best remembered for introducing the bias cut — cutting skirts and complete dresses on the cross of the fabric was a wonderful new way of achieving just the right degree of body-cling and soft flare so important to the growing emphasis on sex appeal in fashion at the end of the 20s.

Throughout history fashion has shown off the curves of the female figure with varying degrees of modesty and daring. Sometimes, breasts, waists and hips have been given equal emphasis. At other times, one or two areas have been highlighted as the most enticing features of women's sex appeal — the so-called erogenous zones.

Admiration for the boyishly-slim figure of the 20s was the most radical change for centuries. Apart from in private, scantily-covered, bare-limbed women had been unknown since the earliest civilisations. Now, legs and feet were the centre of attention as never before and an undeniable focus of sex appeal.

The impact of legs on show for the first time can hardly be overstated, following such a long period in which covering up the female form from top-to-toe had been so obsessive. In many ways, it was even more sensational than the mini skirts of the 60s which took the original concept of 'legginess' one stage further. Both of these periods had more shock value than the third era of leg show in the late 80s and early 90s, which revived mini and micro lengths for a second time in less than a generation.

For many men in the 20s, the sight of so many confident young women with good legs, wearing smooth-fitting, flesh-coloured, seamed silk stockings, showing their knees and thighs as they got out of cars or sat on trains and buses, represented the allure of glamour dressing in its most potent form.

Shoe styles, in keeping with the mood of fashion, were adding their own kind of glamour. Day shoes were neat and feminine-looking with oval toes and straight, high heels. The classic court shoe was the everyday basic, but newer-looking were the more dressy, slender-heeled sandals with ankle- or T-straps in reptile skins, soft kid, suede or satin. Shoes were immaculately presented − matt fabrics were always well-brushed and leather buffed to a high gloss. Evening shoes were more feminine still with even greater use of delicate, strappy designs. The straps were sometimes plaited or made of satin ribbon and crossed over like ballet pumps. Other styles were dotted with glitter and fastened with fancy gold, silver or diamanté buckles. The sides and heels of shoes were also sometimes decorated with tiny gold flecks or diamanté tips. Gold and silver kid 'charleston' sandals were very popular and versatile for teaming up with a wide range of evening dresses. Other shoes were covered

with fabric to match a particular dress; alternatively, dresses in plain velvet, satin or chiffon were worn with patterned shoes, making pretty high-heeled sandals covered in glittering brocade the most eyecatching feature of the outfit.

The ever-growing, later 20th-century preoccupation with body culture and a youthful image started in the 20s. It developed as part of the emancipation of post-war women. The delicate, cossetted, Edwardian lady sitting under her lace-trimmed parasol was relegated to a grandma image and was completely outdated by a far more active, vital woman, who often took part in several sports − tennis, swimming and astride horseriding were all popular daytime activities, usually followed in the evening with energetic dances such as the charleston, the black bottom and the shimmy.

Body-shaping exercises, dieting, and regular visits to the newly popular 'beauty parlours' for body and facial massages, together with help and advice on make-up, were all a part of striving to attain the ideal of slender youthfulness. Cosmetic surgery was in its infancy but the facelift became available and, for the not-so-young, it was an expensive and daring new option.

Sunbathing was growing ever more popular and was rarely thought of as a health hazard. Suntanned young couples, displaying their well-proportioned figures in briefer, better-fitting swimsuits showed − over six decades ago − that cultivating a good-looking body was as important as choosing the right clothes to enhance it. A happy-looking, attractive, young Joan Crawford, photographed in 1929, sitting on the beach, newly-married to an equally cheerful, handsome, young Douglas Fairbanks Jr − both wearing simple one-piece swimsuits − captured very well an early example of glamour projected without the help of stylised hair, lavish make-up and expensive designer clothes.

Relaxed attitudes towards glamour for men as well as women, with some parallel trends in fashion, beauty techniques and body care, unremarkable in recent decades,

The casually chic, fashion-conscious
'spectator sports' outfit became an
established way of dressing.

MONTLHÉRY
Ensemble de sport de MARCEL ROCHAS

would have been unacceptable to many people in the 20s. Women's fashion had undergone a revolution, but style direction for men, although changed after the First World War, was still post-Victorian and discussions and advice on glamorising men would have been subject to considerable ridicule and generally considered unmanly and effete.

Young men in particular have always been concerned with their appearance and the image they project. In some periods of history, the style-conscious 'peacocking' of men, with lavish displays of ornamentation, extreme fashion and overt sexiness in dress, has rivalled and, at times, exceeded women's. Examples across the centuries range from medieval men in tights with featured codpieces and shoes so pointed that they curved upwards, to Stuart cavaliers bedecked in large-brimmed, feather-laden hats, and tunics and breeches heavily trimmed with lace, frills and bows. A century later, the dandy emerged with his bouffant-powdered hair, perfume, heavy make-up and the obligatory painted-on beauty spot. He, in turn, was succeeded by the swaggering Regency buck in high-waisted cutaway coat and skin-tight pantaloons tucked into high leather boots, edged with gold braid and swinging gold tassels.

In the early part of the 20th century, men followed fashion in a much more clandestine way, with style shown in subtle forms and imagery displayed within the bounds of long-established convention.

The archetypal English gentleman, elegantly dressed in a confident but conservative way by world-famous, London bespoke tailors, shirt-makers, hatters and specialists in handmade shoes and boots, had been acknowledged as the pinnacle of men's stylishness in the middle of the 19th century and remained so until the Second World War. Fashion changes evolved slowly – even the slightly dandyish trends, popular at the turn of the century, had faded out by the 1910s. During the 20s and 30s, English style was at its most classic and understated, with great care and attention

given to dressing the individual client in high-quality, perfectly-fitted, flattering clothes, rather than promoting a strong 'designer look'.

After the First World War, there was some rejection of over-formality and stiffness in menswear by the younger generation, possibly as a reaction to having spent several years in military uniform which, in many cases, had followed on from a disciplined Edwardian childhood and adolescence.

Social life was less rigid and more spontaneous and this was reflected in young men's attitudes towards clothes. There was a general easing of fit with lower-cut, softer-collared shirts, less structured jackets – often double-breasted – looser trousers and lighter-weight, lace-up shoes in simple styles. The more extreme image of men's fashion in the 20s, with large-brimmed trilby hats, wide-revered suits, fancy-patterned sweaters and two-toned shoes (frequently portrayed as a romantic look in later decades) had a fairly mixed reception in its original form and was often thought of as being in questionable taste, or even brash. It was worn only by a minority, mainly undergraduates, show business personalities and men connected with the arts.

Although glamour and fashion-consciousness became noticeably less restrained and repressed later in the century, particularly in the 60s and 70s, much of the established structure of what constitutes appropriate dressing for men has remained intact and rooted in basic ideas which evolved in the last century. In fact, conformist dressing was somewhat revived in the career-orientated, 'yuppie' 80s and today, in the last decade of the century, despite a growing industry centred on men's appearance, a really radical and unashamedly exuberant 'new age' in men's fashion has yet to arrive.

The main shift in fashion interest for men in the 20s focused on legs, just as in women's fashion, but unlike the preoccupation with how much leg should be shown off with skimpy fit and up-and-down hemlines, the controversy for men was how much fabric should be used to cover them up. In the first two decades of this century, men's trouser shapes were quite slim and tapered, even sportswear knickerbockers were only moderately wide – in the 20s they ballooned into baggy *plus-fours* and Oxford undergraduates popularised very loose-fitting, wide-legged trousers. These 'Oxford bags' measured as much as 26 inches (66cm) round the trouser bottoms. The extremes of both styles were worn only by a few, but their influence led to easier, fuller-cut trousers being accepted as the norm by the end of the decade, even for the conventional business suit of the time.

The area where men's and women's fashion was at its most similar was in hairdressing – styles for both sexes were short, sleek and groomed, and with the short-back and-sides of the 'Eton crop' they coincided exactly. It was a truly 'unisex' style, 40 years before the description was generally used; remarks were made and cartoons drawn pointing out the similarities between the back views of young men and newly-trousered young women and the difficulties of distinguishing between the sexes. In the late 60s and early 70s, the similarities in how some young couples looked from the back was again mused over. This time it was because the long hairstyles so popular with young men were criticised for looking too feminine.

The 1920s saw the most radical changes in the meaning of women's fashion and the way they looked since the years immediately following the French Revolution. The changes for men were very modest in comparison and the scope for glamour reached a low point in the history of men's costume. It was confined mainly to traditional, special-occasion dressing, such as equestrian events – showjumping, foxhunting and polo – or to the full-dress uniforms worn by regular army and naval officers. The one area where scope for extrovert, fantasy and wide-ranged glamour-dressing was really opening up, however, was in the fast-growing world of cinema.

The film industry – with Hollywood as its centre – had developed rapidly during the 1910s and was well-established by the late 20s; a seemingly limitless future appeared to lie ahead with the arrival of 'talkies'. Cinemas were opening all over the world and small towns throughout America and Europe already had several local 'picture palaces' which were habitually attended by a large part of the population two or three times a week.

Hollywood, realising the powerful influence that films had on the public's imagination, promoted actors and actresses as 'the stars of the silver screen'. When a film was clearly aimed at promoting a male star, the screen story was frequently set as a historical adventure and romance, allowing for plenty of uninhibited, macho action combined with the sex appeal of the star wearing flamboyant, body-fitting period costume.

Rudolph Valentino, the most prolific male sex symbol of the 20s, played nearly all his best-known roles in period costume; even in his famous role as 'Son of the Sheik', although vaguely set in the contemporary time, his costumes verged on fancy-dress. He played a daring, dashing half-Arab/half-European and his mixed cultures and nationalities were reflected in his main outfit with a pseudo-Arab flowing headdress, embroidered shirt open to the chest and wide cummerbund hung with daggers – below which everything was 'European gentleman', with well-tailored jodhpurs and immaculately-polished riding boots.

The available glamour-source of costume roles was also popular for female stars but they were not relied on in the same way for highlighting the star's fantasy image and sex appeal. In the early 20s, women had often been portrayed in over-simplistic forms; the good-girl heroines played by Mary Pickford and Lillian Gish were too unbelievably pure, innocent and sugary-sweet, while bad girl vamps, played by Pola Negri, were darkly melodramatic and totally wicked

temptresses. By the late 20s, however, Hollywood's way of presenting women's images had started to mature. It was still stagey and unreal by later standards but it was more credible and projected a variety of contemporary role models for women to identify with.

Already a big star in the late 20s, Greta Garbo's haunting beauty and chiselled features made her the most mysterious, remote and wanly romantic European. Her style of dress endorsed this image with slouchy, dipping-brim hats (which became known as 'Garbo hats'), turned-up collared top-coats, drapey blouses and floaty, wispy evening dresses discreetly dotted with glitter.

In complete contrast, Clara Bow, the famous 'It' girl, was shown as a much more extrovert personality – breezy,

energetic and potentially naughty without being really bad. She epitomised the bold, newly-emancipated American woman, full of pep and get-up-and-go, all of which was reflected in her style which incorporated a bouncy bobbed hairstyle, frankly made-up face heavily emphasising her big eyes, and jokey sailor-pants outfits or girlish dresses with short, pleated skirts worn with shiny, strappy, tap-style shoes.

Joan Crawford's early screen roles were very different from the dramatic ones she became famous for in the 30s and 40s at the height of her career. In the 1928 film, *Our Dancing Daughters*, she was successfully cast as a charleston-mad jazz baby, a brittle good-time-girl, dazzling young men and shocking the older generation in her skimpy, body-

Far left: Rudolph Valentino, in his dashing costume roles, particularly *The Sheik*, was an adored sex symbol to many women.

Left: Although female curves remained unemphasised, fit moved a little closer to the body and hemlines began to lengthen.

revealing chemise dress decorated with glittering embroidery and fringing.

Norma Shearer projected the more sophisticated characteristics to which some women aspired, with a classy American image – cool, but with romantic inclinations. Less remote than Garbo, she portrayed the elegant, socially-sporty woman in her pristine tennis whites or custom-made, wide-topped jodhpurs, who changed into discreet, chic day outfits worn with designer hats and expensive furs for smart lunch appointments. The same characterised woman could be fun at parties, but always with a degree of restraint, and Norma Shearer looked wonderfully glowing and unruffled in evening dresses of bias-cut crêpe or slinky satin, topped for entrance and exit scenes with matching satin wraps or swirling, fur-trimmed cloaks; her clothes were glossy-magazine-fashion rather than Hollywood-costume-department.

Showing off high fashion, with its newly emerging glamour looks, in fictional, high-society settings, quickly became very popular with the cinema's growing audiences of women from every kind of background and culture. Not many could afford the expensive designs shown on the screen, but they enjoyed the glamorous presentation and absorbed the influence which affected the types of clothes they made or bought.

Hollywood – quick to appreciate its potential for promoting fashion – adapted the latest design directions from Paris to suit their most successful box office superstars. It became an important new media channel for popularising fashion trends to the masses, which developed even further in the following decade as Hollywood reached the zenith of its influence. Many women preferred to be led by their favourite film star's looks, hairstyles and choice of clothes rather than directly following the dictates of dress designers, fashion magazines and newspaper reports.

Most people look back on the 20s with affection, as a

Far left: Norma Shearer in 1929 – groomed, vampishly made-up and already a Hollywood superstar.

Left: Ronald Coleman was often cast as a romantic, gentlemanly hero, and his slim, precisely-shaped moustache was widely copied.

Above: The young Jean Harlow at the beginning of her Hollywood career, soon to become the 'platinum blonde' of the early 30s.

period when society was relatively free from the daunting problems which overshadowed so many of the other decades. The decorative arts and entertainment flourished in the receptive atmosphere of the time, which welcomed the new and the modern and had the financial resources to sponsor and patronise them.

Fortunes were made quickly in the 'boom years', particularly in America, and many of the established rich increased their wealth and continued to enjoy living in the grand style with palatial homes staffed by armies of servants. There was still a leisured, international way of life with men and women who, unlike some of their children and grandchildren, felt no sense of guilt, inferiority or lack of status because they didn't work. The finance needed to support their lifestyles had been available for so long that a serious approach to making it was not often a preoccupation.

Clothes-buying by the style-conscious super-rich was a leisured ritual. Men went to their London tailors and shoemakers while women bought at the couturiers' which, at that time, catered almost exclusively for individual clients with their international social life that required many different types of clothes for a variety of cities, resorts and climates, and for the much more categorised 'occasion' way of dressing that was still habitually followed and frequently called for several changes of outfit each day.

The couture houses, led by Paris, were at the peak of their scope and success. They often occupied entire elegant period buildings in exclusive streets and were dedicated to the presentation of a designer's individual style in the most luxurious, pampered and glamorous way. Halls, reception rooms and showrooms were impressively furnished with antique or modern art-deco furniture and decorated in soft, neutral colours – pale pearl-grey, blue-grey or peach-tinted beige. There were heavily-draped satin curtains, walls of mirror-glass, sumptuous carpets and huge bowls of expensive flowers, the smell of which mingled with the designer's perfumes regularly sprayed around the rooms.

Clients were always given the services of their own *vendeuse*, an elegant, cultured woman with a developed sense for advising on the best choice of clothes from the designer's collection for the individual and her way of life;

Left: Cocoon-shaped evening wraps
and dresses with fluttering hemlines
were among the most appealing of
early glamour images.

As the Roaring 20s gave way to the
Sophisticated 30s, evening dress
designers anticipated the more
figure-fitting lines of the new
decade.

they were in constant attendance during the customer's visit, sitting with her during the fashion show and arranging and supervising all the fittings that were considered necessary during the making of the selected designs.

Showing the designer's collection could take up to two hours, starting with suits and coats and then moving on to dresses for morning, afternoon, cocktail parties and formal and informal evening occasions, all of which were shown in great variety.

At the turn of the decade, the effects of the Depression on the fortunes of many of the clients reduced the scope for the couture houses; fashion shows were modified and fewer staff (expert fitters, tailors, furriers, embroiderers and seamstresses) were required to produce the collections. The basic format, however, continued and later expanded again but was never revived on such a lavish scale.

By the end of the 20s, endings as well as beginnings had affected lifestyles and new concepts had been established, most notably glamour in fashion which, although subject to many changes and interpretations, became a traditionally-admired quality in looks throughout the following decades.

Far left: Classic drapery and sinuous lines were features of the more glamorous, elegant styles at the end of the 20s.

Left: Joan Crawford, surrounded by admirers, played a modern 'jazz baby' in the 1928 film *Our Dancing Daughters*.

The Sophisticated 30s

SECTION ONE The force of world events in the early 30s, the economic slump following the stock market crash of October 1929, combined with growing militancy in many parts of the world, caused a sobering and quicker-than-usual change of mood from one decade to the next. Although more controlled by international co-operation, a similar situation took place 60 years later when the aspirations of the late 80s had to be revised in the altered circumstances of the early 90s.

Opposite: Slinky evening dresses looked wonderfully chic and sophisticated on the very slim.

The fashionable world of the 30s reacted to more serious times with a distinct change in attitude. The youthful optimism which had characterised the giddy, reckless 20s was replaced by escapism in the more threatening atmosphere of the new decade.

Glamour looks for women were more sophisticated and mature – the trend away from the straight, boyish lines of the 20s continued and the classic, womanly curves of the breasts, waist and hips were clearly shown again for the first time since the early years of the century. They were to remain emphasised by fashion until the late 1950s.

In the early 30s, showing off the female form was a totally different concept to the rather matronly and uphol-stered-looking curves so fashionable in the Edwardian period. The newly-admired 'streamlined' figure was slim and lithe, and yet perfectly proportioned and rounded. It was a daunting ideal for many women. The new willowy silhouette was uncompromisingly figure-conscious, with bodices that were softly shaped over the breasts and fitted into trim, belted waistlines, and long thigh- and hip-clinging skirts showed even the slightest bulge or hint of heaviness. To achieve the all-important, snake-hipped curves, many women wore the new latex girdles and stockings that rolled over and finished just below the knees (long stockings fastened to suspender belts often showed through the fine dress fabrics of the period). For women fortunate enough to have the right shape, the new fashions looked stunning. They were flattering, feminine and sexy, with material that was sinuous and supple, wrapping, draping and outlining the body without contorting or exaggerating it.

John Cavanagh, one of London's best-known couture designers of the 1950s, started his career in the 30s, at the house of Molyneux, who was enjoying even more acclaim than he had experienced in the 20s, and opened – with great success – a London branch of his couture house at the height of the Depression. Molyneux's style suited the new mood of

sophisticated glamour and Cavanagh remembers him continually emphasising the importance of designing clothes that flattered women; it was the simple basis of his fashion philosophy. Considerable thought and time were spent to find the most effective use of fabrics; a particular material was draped and arranged on a model girl in front of mirrored walls and – to ensure that a fabric moved attractively – Edward Molyneux even danced to and fro with one of his models, who was pinned into a mocked-up version of a new evening dress line.

Fashionable clothes were more detailed and dressy than the rather uniform designs of the previous decade. The couturiers presented collections with distinctive, individual lines and themes; one designer would feature classical-style drapery, another a Chinese influence with mandarin-

Above: American-born designer Mainbocher putting the final touches to one of his slender, long-skirted day dresses of the early 30s.

collared tunics, while others would show a revival of softly-flared peplums and bustle-backs, or – in complete contrast – embroidered, short, Spanish-style bolero jackets worn over long, body-fitting dresses.

Chanel, who had been famed a few years earlier for her casual cardigan jackets, sweater tops and easy, short skirts, promoted more formal, stylised fashions, including her glamorously-elegant velvet suits which featured wider shoulders, jewelled buttons, narrow waists and slim, calf-length skirts, teamed with matching velvet and satin berets decorated with jewelled clips to match the buttons on the suit.

As the 30s progressed, there was a growing trend for more strongly-stated silhouettes with broader shoulder lines and – from about 1933 onwards – puffed-out, gathered

Above: Schiaparelli, the important new designer of the decade, appraises her more strongly-stated, figure-shaped and peplum-backed 1933 silhouette.

sleeve-heads and square, padded shoulders became the characteristic fashion features of the decade. They were not, however, as aggressively square as the boxy lines of the early 40s, or as obviously bulbous as the power-dressed fashions of the mid-1980s. Elsa Schiaparelli, the important new designer-name of the 30s, is often credited with having started the fashion for big shoulders and more angular lines. She certainly introduced a new range of influences on fashion.

Chanel, Schiaparelli's arch rival, is reputed to have described her as 'the Italian artist who makes clothes' – although probably meant in a detrimental way, it was, in fact, a valid comment and one Schiaparelli might have been quite happy to accept. She came from an academic and artistic background and had been interested in poetry, painting and design from an early age. She had spent time as an antiques dealer before entering the fashion world.

Schiaparelli's interest in the arts gave her designs a very novel, individual slant and, sometimes, a lighthearted touch of humour. She fastened some of her suit jackets with buttons shaped like lips, hearts, stars, moons or old coins and showed some crazy-looking hats, including those shaped like a shoe and a dangling sock. She used colour in daring, unconventional ways; her famous shade of cerise pink, 'shocking pink', teamed with black or navy, bright blue and green together and vivid orange with dark brown, although unremarkable today, were considered a modern artist's colour palette rather than couture fashion when 'Schap' first launched them in her collections.

She was friendly with many of the avant-garde artists of the period and admired the works of Jean Cocteau and Salvador Dali. Schiaparelli expressed the influence of modern art and the escapist tendencies of the time in the most graphic way with her jackets and evening coats, decorated with surrealistic prints and embroideries.

Alix, later to become Madame Gres, was another well-

Far right: Soft lines and pale colours were the style features of many dressy day outfits.

Right: The low back, combined with clinging fit, emphasised a new and daring body-conscious style of dressing.

known designer with an affiliation to the art world; her style of designing, however, was very different to Schiaparelli's. She had trained as a sculptor before becoming a couturier and her unique use of fabric had a sculptured quality. She became famous for her draped and pleated dresses in crêpe, silk jersey and chiffon, which were clearly inspired by the robes worn in Ancient Greece and Rome, or by the traditional wrapping of the sari and the sarong. Her

die neue
linie

Juni 19

ARPKE

The long dinner suit was one of the
newest fashions of the decade –
none was more elegant than this
Molyneux design of 1934.

superbly-draped, or delicately-pleated, long, white evening dresses were truly timeless classics and could have been worn to equal effect in any of the following six decades.

Paris has often been called the capital of fashion and for centuries it has been a centre for creating stylish costumes and promoting French textiles. The rich fabrics and extravagant designs worn at the French court were copied and adapted throughout Europe; even during the Napoleonic Wars, French silks and embroideries were daringly smuggled into England, via the rugged coastlines of Devon and Cornwall, to appear later as a society beauty's much-envied ball dress, or tailored into expensive waistcoats for Regency dandies.

Paris has always attracted artistic talent from all over the world. Charles Worth, the first internationally-known Paris couturier in the 19th century, renowned for his strikingly elegant designs and his exclusive clientele, which included the Empress Eugenie, was an Englishman from Lincolnshire.

By the 1930s, Paris couture was multi-national and consisted of French, Italian, Russian, Spanish and Irish designers and a successful new American — Mainbocher — originally from Chicago. Before opening his fashion house, he had been a journalist, a fashion artist and, for a while, Fashion Editor and then Editor of French *Vogue*. His style of designing was a little like that of Molyneux, understated and consciously flattering, but with slightly more boldness in his use of colour, patterns and line. His most famous client was Wallis Simpson — in 1937, she chose him to design her elegant, subtly-draped, long crêpe wedding dress and her trousseau. Her own sense of style was perfect for Mainbocher's designs — she suited his slim-fitting, uncluttered lines and was always immaculately groomed, glossy and faultlessly presented. Of course, she made an even more dazzling impression when accompanied by her famous and glamorous escort, firstly when he was the Prince of Wales, then —

briefly — King of England and later her husband, the Duke of Windsor.

The leading couturiers' more individualistic approach to designing offered women a wider range of options in fashion. Although day clothes became more formal, with their fitted lines, longer skirts and more considered silhouettes, they had to remain practical enough for women's active day-to-day lives in the fourth decade of the 20th century. No such limitations, however, applied to evening wear and women enjoyed a decade of gorgeously impractical evening dresses.

When shorter skirts first arrived in the 1910s, and throughout the ups and downs of hemlines during the 20s, day and evening lengths were usually about the same. However, with the elongated silhouette of the early 30s, day lengths fell to lower-calf, but evening dress dropped to ankle- or floor-length for the first time since the early 1910s, remaining so until the present day, despite many a rise and fall in daytime hemlines. With really long, flowing skirts and body-fitting silhouettes the scope for evening dress design was more extensive and gave full rein to 30s glamour-dressing.

The backless evening dress was one of the most daring new fashions of the early 30s. Often made in black or white slinky satin or fluid crêpe, it looked its best on suntanned young women with faultless figures. The back was cut out almost to the waistline and the material for the front part of the bodice was taken from the side seams like two attached scarves and crossed and softly draped up over the breasts to fasten round the neck in a halter-style; the skirt clung to the hips like a second skin and flared gently from the thighs to touch or trail on the ground in a fluted trumpet-shape. Glittering earrings and bracelets were added and the outfit was topped with a white or silver-fox cape or a pair of foxes wrapped round the neck and flung over the shoulders.

Later in the decade, a new, equally sensational, body-revealing evening-dress line was introduced – the strapless, boned bodice designed to push out the breasts, mould the torso and pull in the waist. It was like a modernised corset made in the dress fabric and on show as an integral part of the dress. Strapless tops were sometimes designed with narrow skirts but were more generally used with very full skirts gathered or flared from the waistline. Some tops and skirts were effectively styled in contrasting colours and fabrics, white lace bodices with floaty skirts made from layers of black chiffon, or black satin tops teamed with dark red skirts in rustling taffeta.

Flattering black velvet became a favourite fabric for full-skirted dresses with tiny strapless bodices, styled into a heart-shaped line over the breasts. To add further allure, some dresses had black chiffon joined to the black velvet, adding a transparent top half to the bodice, covering the shoulders up to the neck and the arms down to the wrists in narrow chiffon sleeves. It was such a successful combination of body show and sensual fabrics that Hollywood soon claimed the style, and chiffon-topped evening gowns became the standard film-star dresses of the 30s, 40s and 50s.

Gold lamé was an even more overtly sexy and theatrical fabric, popularised in the 30s and Hollywood-endorsed. Lamé was nearly always used for very figure-hugging dresses with tight ruched bodices and narrow slit skirts draped onto one hip. Fashion and film magazines often described them, rather fancifully, as 'columns of molten gold'.

The appeal of 1930s fashion – inventiveness, charm, desirability and glamour – has endured for over half a century. Influences and ideas from the 30s have been repeated, revised and adapted many times over the decades. What made them so special? The times and lifestyles, despite the Depression years, were more receptive to glamorous, sophisticated clothes. The theatre and the cinema promoted

them and 'occasion' and evening dressing was still considered important and was widely followed. But perhaps even more significant were the creative talents of the designers; their calibre, experience and credentials were often impressively high which, together with artistic and social awareness, helped them to develop their individual style and fulfil their potential.

Madge Garland, who had been a Fashion Editor of English *Vogue* in the 30s and a part of the international fashion scene, was Professor of Fashion at the Royal College of Art, in London, from the late 40s to the mid-50s. She continually encouraged her students to broaden their interests and absorb influences from a wide range of creative talents – classical, modern and decorative art, the theatre, dance crazes and social life – in the conviction that it would enrich them and expand and develop their flair for fashion designing as it had many of the successful designers she had known in the 30s.

Three smart ladies in dressy hats and furs – essential glamour accessories throughout the decade.

Striking, stylish hats were very much a part of sophisticated urban fashion images.

Nostalgia, like escapism, is always more appealing during uncertain times. As succeeding generations in the 20th century have been confronted with so many turbulent national and international events, nostalgia for the seemingly more secure and romantic world of the recent past has been a recurring theme. Its comforting charm was least popular during the 1900s, 20s and 60s, the decades with the greatest confidence in their own times.

In the 20s, 19th-century and Edwardian fashions were often ridiculed for having been fussy, over-elaborate, ultra-feminine and even sexist in restricting women's emancipation and were thought to have been laid to rest with no place in an irreversibly modern world.

Victorian fashion was viewed quite differently in the 30s. It was the turn of the 1920s 'modern' styles to be considered passé and for some of the more traditional ideas of the earlier periods to be reinstated. There was much talk in women's magazines about fashion 'getting back to normal' and 'settling down', and of the joys of women rediscovering their femininity and cultivating a more beguiling female image. Although the Victorian revival was an important trend throughout the decade, it was adapted to the pace, lifestyles and glamour ideals of the 30s; fashionably made-up faces, obviously-dyed hair and slim, rounded figures helped to keep the revivalist fashion within the context of influences rather than total recall.

Make-up in the 30s became more mature-looking. It was quite heavy by later standards, with a growing use of foundation colour, but more thought and care were given to glamorising individual looks rather than superimposing rather doll-like painted faces. Eyebrows continued to be finely plucked and pencilled in, eyes were clearly outlined, but the application was more flattering. Lips became the most emphasised focal point of make-up – little pursed lips were completely out of date and were replaced by the fashion for large, full mouths – if women felt their lips were too thin,

an enlarged shape was drawn on and filled in with deep red lipstick.

Joan Crawford made the strong, full mouth an important feature of her look and the 'Joan Crawford mouth' became one of the most characteristic and easy-to-achieve make-up ideals of the decade.

Hair was grown much longer and worn in more elaborate styles. Even the easy-to-wear bob lengthened to the shoulders and was neatly turned under in a medieval pageboy style. The front of the hair was parted at the side or in the centre and softly waved over the temples. Alternatively, the side hair was pinned up off the face, allowing the back to fall smoothly down onto the shoulders. Garbo adopted the pageboy bob, countless admiring women followed her lead and it was soon renamed the 'Garbo Bob'.

The influence of the superstars was so great that they could make any fashion a part of their own persona; Jean Harlow, one of the famous sex symbols of the era, dyed her hair the palest shade of blonde and quickly became known as the 'Platinum Blonde'. It was another achievable Hollywood 'film star look' and Jean Harlow lookalike blondes soon multiplied.

As an alternative to hairstyles that fell down to the shoulders, there was a parallel trend for taking hair up, and fashion magazines promoted the 'upswept look' with styles that were pinned into neat rolls, waves and curls at the back and sides. Later in the decade, as the trend for Victorian and Edwardian influences intensified, much longer hair was piled on top of the head in deep, stylised waves and curls, held in place with combs or arranged with pinned pompadour fronts, rolled or turned under at the back and held in place with mesh snoods.

Vivien Leigh's unforgettably vivid portrayal of Scarlett O'Hara in *Gone with the Wind* strongly endorsed fashion's romance with 19th-century hairstyles and extravagant clothes, which was at its height when the film was launched in 1939. To ensure that the film's lavish costumes appealed to the mass cinema audiences of the time, Hollywood cleverly adapted the period styles to suit the film stars' contemporary looks and figures.

Hat styles, like hair, became more elaborate and varied. Fashion reacted away from the cloche, which had been dominant for so long, with a wide range of shapes and designs; the only limitation for the new styles was that they had to work with the more contrived approach to arranging hair. Hats were chosen to suit hairstyles, or hair was dressed to complement hats. Design influences were international, covering the traditional, the ethnic and the historical and included French berets, Tyrolean hats trimmed with feathers, cossack hats, fezzes, coolie hats and turbans, together with many revived turn-of-the-century styles.

Some of the most flattering designs in the first half of the 30s were the small, side-tilted pillbox hats, delicately trimmed with ribbons and veiling, and the wide, dipping-brim, 'mother of the bride' styles in striped silk or fine, two-toned straw.

In the second half of the 30s, as fashionable looks became even more dressy, small, very feminine, forward-tilted doll hats were introduced. Made in brushed felt, satin or velvet, they often had miniature crowns and brims trimmed with soft, curling feathers or ruched ribbons; alternatively, the same shape was made from a ring of draped chiffon or silver fox, and the designs were usually covered in spotted or net veiling and were held on the head with an elastic band, concealed in a deeply-rolled, swept-up hairstyle. The elaborate, stylised hats and hairstyles, combined with the immaculate artifice of late 1930s make-up and worn with square-shouldered, tailored suits and fox furs, represented one of the most urban and sophisticated fashion images of the decade.

The trend for decoration and embellishment affected fashion from top to toe and shoes were no exception. The greater variety of styles and lines of day and evening clothes required a wide range of more carefully chosen shoes. Prettier, higher-cut designs complemented longer skirts and helped to compensate for losing the impact of showing off the legs. Draped silk bands, soft bows or ornamental buckles were used on high-fronted town shoes, or they were laced over the arch of the foot with silk or fancy cord laces. Small cutouts like stencil patterns, or tiny perforated dots, decorated the fronts and sides of some styles, others featured rows of top-stitching or very narrow strips of leather on suede, as decorative effects on toe and heel caps.

Later in the decade, fashion interest focused even more intensely on inventive shoe design. Strappy sandals with high heels became popular for day as well as evening wear and inspired very new-looking styles with open toes, sling backs, platform soles and high or wedge heels. The young ultra-fashion-conscious loved the new designs – they became the glamour shoes of the late 30s and early 40s, and later the inspiration for the much more extreme platforms and wedges of the early 1970s.

The enduring image of fashion in the 30s, for many people, is most strongly represented by the film stars' clothes. Hollywood epitomised glamour and stylish dressing and commercialised it in a way that had never been known before; it became, and has remained, synonymous with the superstars' promoted looks, make-up, hairstyles, clothes and even catch-phrases and mannerisms, and reached its peak in the 1930s, the high point in glamour's 'golden age'.

Indeed, Hollywood's influence was phenomenal; crowds packed cinemas every week, 20 000 000 in Britain and over 80 000 000 in the USA alone. The film stars were studied and often slavishly copied – they were idols, 20th-century gods and goddesses. The cinema was a fantasy dreamworld where people could escape from the Depression and the growing threat of war, and watch unbelievably good-looking people with sex appeal and cultivated cool, in magnificent homes, leading lives full of drama, fun and romance.

Spectacular musicals, Busby Berkeley's ingenious, elaborate sequences featuring teams of smiling, pretty girls in long white evening dresses playing white grand pianos, or bathing beauties diving into enormous swimming pools and forming complicated flower shapes through synchronised swimming, have become cinema classics.

Fred Astaire and Ginger Rogers' lighthearted, romantic musicals captured the seductive appeal of escapism as Fred, immaculately dressed in wing-collared shirt, bow tie and tails, and Ginger, deliciously feminine in yards of floaty chiffon edged with ostrich feathers, danced harmoniously to 30s hits such as 'Night and Day' and 'Let's Face the Music and Dance'.

Hollywood, supremely confident in its vast earning capacity, spent huge amounts of money on lavish sets and clothes, the costs of which, if translated into today's equivalent value, would almost certainly be prohibitive for the film makers of the 90s.

Designing clothes for the major stars of the 30s was a serious and professional business; in the highly competitive studio and star system it was no longer enough for designers to simply adapt the latest international trends. They had to be able to project, enhance and individualise the star's image and minimise any defects in looks, size and shape.

Hollywood fashions needed to be strongly stated and have greater direct appeal than the famous couturiers' more traditional approach to designing for the 'real', albeit affluent, lives of their clients. Film clothes required eye-catching lines, photogenic colours and fabrics, and designs with obvious sex appeal. Some of the most famous Paris names, including Chanel and Schiaparelli, were commissioned to design for the movies but they were not a great success – their couturier style did not transfer well onto the screen and lacked impact and film-star appeal. Hollywood's own designers were much more successful and some of them became famous in their own right.

Adrian, who had a long career with MGM, was one of the best-known names; he designed Garbo's outfits for most of her films, including *Queen Christina*, *Camille* and *Ninotchka*. He also designed the clothes for *The Women* which featured actresses as hard-edged, ultra-smart New Yorkers of the late 30s. His styles were among the most high-fashion ever shown in the movies, and his peplum suits, draped and bustle-backed dresses and forward-tilted hats were well up to the *Vogue* and *Harpers Bazaar* standards of the time.

Adrian helped to popularise heavily-padded shoulder lines. Width at the top gave the illusion of slimmer hips and a fashionably willowy line to film stars with less-than-perfect figures. Many women found that it could do the same for them and shoulder pads remained popular until the late 1940s.

The designs of Adrian did more than just dress the stars well; they had a distinctive style which was as recognisable as those of the many famous Paris designers. He was known for his sharply-tailored suits, striking use of black and white together and in particular for his glamorous glitter embroidery; he used glittering motives as prominent features on dressy day outfits and sophisticated evening dresses, or delicately as discreet sparkle or frosted effects on his romantic ball dresses in white lace, tulle or chiffon.

Adrian became so well-known, particularly in America, that he was able to expand his career and later sell his own up-market fashion ranges direct to the public. Women could buy the exact style of design that they had admired so much on the screen. It was a great success, particularly during the first part of the 40s, when high fashion imports from Europe were no longer available because of the War.

If one superstar had to be nominated as having epitomised 30s glamour, it would have to be Marlene Dietrich. Her *femme fatale* image was a heady mix of

The face of 30s glamour – stylised waves, arched brows and the strong mouth.

sexiness and chic, warmer than fashion magazine elegance, but nevertheless slightly aloof and verging on the unattainable. Her style was Hollywood-cultivated and promoted. In the 1930 film *The Blue Angel*, Dietrich looked plump and rather provincial in her style of dress; it suited the part she played. But it was very different from the sleek siren of a few years later, after she had slimmed down and been immaculately groomed and dressed by Travis Banton, Paramount's talented designer. The 'new' Dietrich was urban and dressy, even in her trouser suits complete with masculine shirt, tie and dipping-brim hat, she still managed to look towny and sophisticated rather than sporty. Her feminine clothes, figure-fitting suits and softly-swathed dresses were worn with flattering hats draped in veiling or trimmed with fur. Fur was greatly used in her outfits; lavish fox coats were pulled casually round her shoulders, or she wore cloth coats with large fur collars and deep cuffs, sometimes teamed with muffs and Russian-style fur hats to give the romanticised look of a pre-revolution Russian aristocrat.

The revived admiration for womanly curves has often been credited to Mae West's success; her figure would certainly not have suited the fashionable ideals of the 20s. She was in her 40s when she became a famous film star and her silhouette was reminiscent of the mature, corsetted figures popular for turn-of-the-century stage stars. Many of her films were, in fact, set at the end of the 19th century, in the so-called 'naughty 90s'.

She was a natural comedienne; her ample curves and somewhat overstated style of dress were probably intended to be camp and a kind of glamour send-up. The public warmed to her personality and image and found it a lighthearted contrast to Hollywood's obsessive pursuit of perfection in film stars' looks.

Most men in the 1930s continued to be reserved and conformist in their appearance and waited for the cinema to promote, and make acceptable, new male glamour images. The film moguls — always sensitive to the changing mood of the times — presented men with a wider and more varied range of role models than in the previous decade.

Dashing period costume was still a popular aspect of the film stars' fantasy appeal, and Errol Flynn was successfully promoted as the rampant young male in his early swashbuckling roles in *Captain Blood*, *The Charge of the Light Brigade* and *Elizabeth and Essex*. Generally, however, costume drama became just a part of the star's repertoire and more emphasis was placed on modern-day hero roles.

Female superstars tended to dominate the escapist movies of the Depression years. These film goddesses were complemented, on and off screen, by suave, sophisticated consorts; faultlessly groomed and immaculately dressed men with charm and wit, they became one of the most fashionable ideals of the decade and were epitomised by stars such as Herbert Marshall, Melvyn Douglas, Ronald Coleman, Fred Astaire and the young Cary Grant, who developed and perfected his smooth image even further in the 40s and 50s.

The standard of presentation required for the glamour image of the urban male sophisticate was very high, and pristine correctness in every detail was considered all-important.

Hairstyles were worn short and ultra-neat, with a definite side or centre parting and, in order to hold its shape and look fashionably shiny, the hair was oiled and combed back or arranged in one or two finger-pressed waves. It was regularly trimmed rather than cut and shaped so that well-groomed men never looked as if they needed a haircut.

Most men were clean shaven and facial hair was limited to slim, precisely-shaped moustaches which were sometimes regarded as a fashion feature. Ronald Coleman's elegant moustache was widely copied and 'the Ronald Coleman' moustache became almost as well known as 'the Joan Crawford' mouth.

Well-dressed men always completed their outfits with a carefully chosen hat. The soft pull-on trilby with various crown and brim shapes, often dipped over one eye, was the everyday favourite. For more formal occasions, bowlers and homburgs, with their stylised dent across the crown and slightly turned-up brims, were considered more appropriate. The correct evening hat was immortalised on film by the ever-dapper Fred Astaire, in the 1935 classic *Top Hat*, with its lead song and dance routine pointing out the importance of 'Top hat, white tie and tails'.

Apart from active sportswear and very casual summer clothes, shirts, ties and tailored garments were habitually worn. Fashionable suits and long topcoats had sharply-tailored lines and, like the women's silhouette, they featured wider, padded shoulders and larger collars and revers. Jackets were cut to give a slight waist indication and a smooth, flat, close-fitting line round the hips. Widish trousers were pressed into knife-edged creases which broke onto highly-polished lace-up shoes – shiny, conventional shoes were an essential part of being well-dressed.

Masculinity for men was as strongly emphasised as the revived femininity for women in the glamour ideals of the 30s. In contrast to the smooth, well-mannered, gentlemanly roles, 'tough guy' characters were also a popular influence. Boxers; gangsters in double-breasted, chalk-striped suits; detectives and news reporters in long trenchcoats and trilby hats, which were kept on indoors, were played by less obviously-handsome but interesting-looking stars, including James Cagney, George Raft, Humphrey Bogart and Spencer Tracey.

A broader, more athletic build was admired and aspired to by many young men. Dramatic-looking black and white photographs showing the well-developed torsos and rippling muscles of athletes in the build-up to the 1936 Berlin Olympics emphasised the new importance given to 'body culture'. Johnny Weissmuller, a former Olympic swimming champion and one of Hollywood's best-known 'Tarzans', was world-famous for his physique and the 'Tarzan image' became an established archetype.

War films and related action-man heroes had been temporarily out of favour during the 20s, in the aftershock of the First World War. By the 30s, a new post-war generation had grown up and the traditional appeal of the macho fighting man was re-established. Commercially successful films featured the strong and manly: daring pilots wearing leather flying helmets, battered leather jackets and riding breeches, and battle-hardened soldiers in mud-stained uniforms.

The glamour of uniforms and the legitimising of aggressive behaviour has always appealed to the basic instincts of some men. Fascist regimes actively encouraged young men into the lethal combination of showy uniforms and a fostering of the warrior instinct. The undeniable smartness of the Nazi military at the Nuremburg Rally of 1934, filmed by Leni Riefenstal for her propaganda classic *The Triumph of Will*, particularly the columns of immaculate, black-uniformed, gleaming jack-booted SS, presented male glamour in one of its most sinister forms with an impact that even Hollywood would have found difficult to match.

Despite the adverse conditions of the time, an elegant and stylish way of living continued until the outbreak of the Second World War in 1939. The clothes and the social life of well-known 'café society' personalities, such as heiress Barbara Hutton and the increasingly famous Mrs Simpson, were regularly reported. When the attractive Princess Marina of Greece married England's Duke of Kent, *Vogue* devoted pages of photographs and fashion drawings to her superbly-elegant wedding dress and trousseau, which were designed by Molyneux.

Dressing for the fashionable life often meant dressing up and floor-length evening dresses were not only habitually

Above: Thirties escapism personified. The famous dancing duo of the decade, Fred Astaire and Ginger Rogers.

Right: The elitist glamour of the uniformed officer, effectively shown here by Gary Cooper, arm protectively round a wistful Joan Crawford.

worn by many more women more frequently – ranging from the society woman driven off by her uniformed chauffeur in a sleek car, to the modest suburbanite travelling to and from the theatre on public transport – they were also considered correct for other specific occasions.

British debutantes, in sweeping white evening dresses, white ostrich feather headdresses and long white gloves, were launched into London's social season when they were presented to the King at daytime ceremonies. Fussy, frilly, flouncy garden party dresses and Ascot dresses for England's famous summer races were also worn ankle- or floor-length and accessorised with large, floppy-brim hats decorated with flowers.

Even more glamorous than those at Ascot were the Paris Langchamps evening races, held on a floodlit course and attended by chic Parisians in full evening dress. Elegant men in white tie and tails accompanied some of Paris's smartest women, many of whom wore one of the new fashions of the 30s – perfect for cool summer evenings – the evening suit. Dressy, fitted jackets in crêpe, featuring embroidery, or satin or lamé revers, were teamed with narrow-moulded, ankle-length skirts slit up to the knee, and these glamour suits were topped with one of the tiny, delicate evening hats that Paris was famed for. They were forward-tilted and made of ribbon, feathers and net, and described in the fashion magazines of the time as 'frou-frou', 'bits of nonsense' and 'flights of fancy'.

Europe's traditional playgrounds, the Italian and French Rivieras, (before the age of mass-travel and unbridled development), were relatively unspoilt and at their peak as the chic haunts of the smart international set. A deep Mediterranean suntan was still a status symbol and St Tropez and its nearby beaches, which became world-famous and sadly over-commercialised in the 60s, were already popular with the style-setters of the 30s. 'St Trop' was enjoyed then as a charming, sleepy fishing village and

Resort- and cruise-wear was more categorised and considered than in the later decades of the century.

an artists' colony. Drinking or eating at L'Escale, the harbourside restaurant, (still well-known today), was a delightful contrast to the grand hotel life of Cannes, Nice and Monte Carlo.

Although holiday clothes were considered simple and casual, luggage for stylish vacations was substantial. Wardrobe trunks, often sent on ahead, as well as numerous suitcases and hatboxes, were needed for the extensive range of clothes. T-shirts, pants, shorts, swimwear, accessories and

NINA RICCI

Above and right: Evening glamour
of the mid-30s, superbly feminine
and flattering with classic drapery
and flowing lines.

NINA RICCI

NINA RICCI

make-up, often today's total holiday requirements, would have been a very small part of a fashionable woman's holiday wear in the 30s, and would probably not have been thought sufficient for even her maid!

Trousers and shorts for women had been introduced during the 20s and were an accepted part of resort-wear by the 30s, but their use was still generally limited to the beach or for sailing. Loose-fitting 'beach-pyjamas', with sailor-type tops and wide, flapping pants, worn with wavy-brim sunhats and round, white-rimmed sunglasses, were a popular beach fashion of the early 30s. However, the basic cut for trousers, for most of the decade, followed the same line as men's, tailored into widish legs with front pleats and sharply-pressed creases.

For wearing around the resorts, shopping, lunching and general sightseeing, most women still wore neatly-presented, designer-style summer suits, dresses and hats in pastel colours or nautical navy and white, sometimes with ships' wheels or anchors embroidered on the revers or pockets.

Sports such as tennis, golf and horseriding always required the correct attire. In the evening, women transformed their appearance and changed into one of their range of pretty, flowing evening dresses in flower printed voile, or striped or polka-dotted organdie, and arranged their hair in one of the new, more elaborate hairstyles.

A similar style was adopted for leisurely sea travel – cruising to exotic parts of the world on luxury liners, dancing to Latin American music under starry night skies and shipboard romances, fantasised and romanticised so frequently in the movies, was a popular holiday ideal.

Most people still crossed the North Atlantic by sea. Five days of pampered, quality living and showing off smart clothes for social life on famous liners like the *Queen Mary* or the *Queen Elizabeth*, and the finale to the trip – sailing past the New York skyline – was probably far more

memorable than a few hours in a supersonic jet.

Age-grouping as a divisional factor in fashion was viewed very differently in the 30s to how it is seen today. The whole spectrum of teenage culture, which was to be so important in the second half of the century, had hardly begun. Parental control was rigid and often strictly enforced; most parents chose their children's clothes, and the wacky, experimental, cult dressing of later generations would never have been allowed. Mothers dressed their teenage daughters in plain-looking blouses and skirts, buttoned-up dresses and

Left: Marlene Dietrich, the nightclub temptress, in body-cling and glitter.

Above: Tyrone Power in the 30s, wearing an elegant suit, shirt and tie, with more than a hint of the Armani menswear look of the 80s.

tailored coats, which they thought suitably demure. For social occasions, adolescent girls were intended to look girlishly 'sweet', in overly pretty 'party frocks' in sugary colours.

Later in the decade, there were stirrings of revolt, as the impact of 'Big Band Swing' music seemed to unite and energize America's teenagers, and 'bobbysoxers' (boys in oversized sweaters, baggy pants, sloppy socks and gymshoes, and girls in tighter sweaters, short, flared skirts, ankle socks and gymshoes) made their presence felt as they 'jived' and 'jitterbugged' to the latest brassy 'swing' records. They were clearly the predecessors of today's streetwise 'rap' kids in their shell-suits and loosely-laced trainers.

Equally dramatic changes have taken place at the other end of the age scale – the over-50s. The later 20th-century preoccupation with glamorising the older woman – and some of the results of rigorous exercise programmes, strict diet and body and facial cosmetic surgery – would have impressed earlier generations. But the most extreme image of the glamorous Californian grandmother of the early 90s, with her shoulder-length mane of hair and wearing a thigh-length, body-clinging lycra dress similar to that of her 18-year-old grand-daughter, would have horrified the women of the 30s.

Today's resolve to fight the aging process with all available means is in total contrast to the attitudes of 60 years ago, when the inevitability of getting older was accepted more passively and there was a gentler approach to combating the effects of time; efforts were made to disguise and soften rather than actively change.

Health farms in their early forms had already started in America and moderate exercise programmes, some sports activity, a light diet and resting, with the emphasis on the latter, were thought to help maintain young looks.

Beauty experts recommended softly-tinted make-up colours – rose shades for lips, lavender eyeshadow and paler

Left and far left: Mainboucher's stunning use of colour and patternings from his spring 1937 collection.

lavender tints for face power and hair rinses.

Fashion magazines offered regular advice on suitable clothes for the 50-plus age group; covering up seemed to be the main guideline. Readers were informed that 'materials have to be handsome' and 'colours distinguished'. *Vogue*, in the early 30s, advised its readers that, 'no woman can get along without tea-gowns', and that, 'floor-length trains and sleeve interest are most becoming to the mature figure'. Displaying beautiful handkerchiefs was also seriously suggested.

Not all women were prepared to accept such 'dowager-

The immaculately-dressed Coco Chanel – always the perfect advertisement for her own fashion philosophy.

like' images and some of the couturiers' smartest customers were in their 50s. Although they followed the latest fashions, they avoided the more extreme lines; they chose instead designs with a soft neckline and a flattering cut. Clothes were never too fitted and, if short skirts were fashionable, they often had theirs made slightly longer; daring low-backed evening dresses were rejected in favour of styles which draped the shoulders in velvet or chiffon, or featured lace inserts and sleeves, all guaranteed to flatter, particularly when accessorised with a pearl choker. Overall, discreet

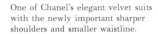

One of Chanel's elegant velvet suits with the newly important sharper shoulders and smaller waistline.

Right and far right: Escapist glamour – ignoring the threatening international situation – showed velvet suits, embroidery and sumptuous furs.

Right: A sleek car was the perfect accessory for the fashionably-dressed young woman-about-town.

Far right: Full-length 'Ascot dresses' were worn at fashionable race meetings.

Modes & Travaux

glamour was preferred for the sophisticated older woman of the 30s.

Jewellery, in keeping with the rest of fashion, was more varied. Platinum (white gold) was modern and looked particularly good on married platinum-blondes in long white evening dresses, who completed their expensive top-to-toe pale look with a fashionable platinum wedding ring.

Necklaces were very popular and new designs complemented the changed silhouettes. The single- or double-stranded long necklace, which had suited the simple chemise dresses of the 20s, didn't work with figure-fitted, broader-shouldered day outfits or moulded, strapless evening dresses. New necklaces, whether single- or multi-stranded, were worn much closer to the base of the neck; styling was more intricate and – at times – almost baroque-inspired with the basic gold shape fashioned into curves, coils, links or leaves and flowers, and decorated with glittering stones, either precious, semi-precious or frankly fake. Matching earrings and bracelets, featuring the same, or part of the same, design theme formed co-ordinating jewellery sets which were at their most effective when accessorising understated black crêpe or velvet dresses and suits.

Affordable diamanté was also widely used to dress up the ever-popular 'little black dress'. Diamanté earrings, particularly diamanté clips, worn singly at the base of a V-neck, or in pairs to hold the corners of a draped 'sweetheart'

Above and right: Hard-edged chic: elaborate, stylised designer hats, upswept hair and the artifice of late-30s make-up.

neckline, became one of the most copied costume jewellery fads of the 30s and early 40s.

The developing fashion trends of the decade – fussy hats, longer hair, broader shoulders and figure-emphasised lines – were all intensified by the leading designers in 1938 and '39. Victorian bonnets tied under the chin, and hair dressed in braided buns were added to the already fashionable range of forward-tilted doll hats and upswept hairstyles. Emphasised curves became more exaggerated, breasts were pushed out with 'uplift' bras, waists pulled in with corselettes and hips highlighted with draped bows or very full, flared skirts, worn over (and sometimes deliberately showing) a glimpse of frilly petticoat. The only concession to practicality

Above: The Paris designers revived the hour-glass figure in their last collections before the Second World War.

was the shortening of daytime hemlines to just below the knee. This, however, might have been a temporary fashion had the Second World War not intervened. In the last Paris collections of 1939, slightly longer lengths were already being shown by some designers to balance wider skirts.

Younger talents, like Pierre Balmain and Christian Dior, were enthusiastically producing designs featuring the revived hourglass figure and ultra-feminine styles. They were established designers in Paris and worked for some of the well-known couture houses but they were not yet stars. After the War, they opened their own fashion houses and their early collections – including Dior's famous 'New Look' of 1947 – were clearly inspired by the fashion directions of the late 30s.

Although the serious events of the 30s have receded into history, interest in the lighter side of the period, its lifestyles and creativity, remains as strong as ever. Reminders of the time are available in a way that would not have been possible in earlier decades. Photography and the cinema have left a wealth of visual memorabilia which has made the style of the decade so familiar to us.

Thirties movies, profiles on the famous stars, and film clips used in news programmes are shown regularly on television. Fashion pictures from the period are used for decoration on posters and greetings cards. Horst's renowned high-fashion photographs decorate the front of T-shirts and are better known today than when they were first featured in *Vogue* and *Harpers Bazaar* over 50 years ago.

Collectors' items from the time – elegant, long-bonneted cars, art-deco and 30s modern furnishings, and feminine clothes and jewellery – always draw admiration; the music, especially ever-popular Gershwin and Cole Porter hits, make the allure of the era even more potent.

The character of war at the end of the 20th century – internationally-sanctioned strikes against aggressors with highly technical weapons, instantaneous worldwide media

Glamour Retained

The Early and Mid-40s

coverage and the ultimate threat of total annihilation by nuclear missiles – would have seemed like a Wellsian vision of the distant future, 50 years ago.

Right: Smart, fashionable hats helped to lift women's morale during the War and austerity years.

Above and right: Fussy, flowery hats worn with precisely-tailored, square-shouldered suits were a popular new glamour format.

Until the atomic bomb was used in 1945, the Second World War, although more modern and extensive than anything known before, had been a traditional war of conquest; country after country in Europe and Asia was subjugated and occupied by military force. In the spring of 1940, however, six months after the European war had begun, serious fighting was still far more limited than most people had expected. The American press called it 'The Phoney War' and the escapism of the 30s lingered on into the new decade as the Paris couturiers presented their spring collections as usual.

With the uncertain future of the European market the new collections were designed to appeal to the unaffected Americans, and enthusiastic press reports noted that over a hundred US buyers had braved the Atlantic and were delighted with the spring fashions, which were described as 'extremely feminine with not the slightest trace of a military influence'.

The Paris designers had softened the more extreme lines of 1939. Shoulders remained wide, waists pulled-in and skirts short, but the more exaggerated, corsetted curves and contrived silhouettes of the previous season, with panniered dresses, Victorian bustles and tightly-draped hobble skirts, were obviously unsuited to the changed times and the available fashion markets.

More of the new designs featured dresses with fuller-cut shirt bodices trimly belted into the waist, or short bolero jackets worn over pretty, feminine-looking blouses tucked into easy-to-wear, flared skirts. Dressy afternoon or cocktail dresses in crêpe or silk jersey, with fitted bodices and slim or unpressed pleated skirts, were often designed with over-skirt effects – the attached fabric was softly draped into apron fronts or swathed to the side and tied like a sarong.

Hat styles also reflected the more gentle fashion trends of 1940. Little, delicately-trimmed, forward-tilted doll hats were still fashionable but newer looking, very girlish, off-

the-face designs – boaters, bonnets and turbans decorated with lifesize tulips and roses and often covered in veiling were also strongly featured and shown with tailored outfits as well as dressy clothes. Fussy, flowery hats worn with precisely-tailored coats, suits and dresses became a popular new glamour format of the 40s. When austerity set in and most women had to make their basic outfits last for several years, teaming them with a new, strongly-stated, pretty hat was a good morale booster and livened up clothes that had become boringly familiar.

High hats, large, inflated berets and towering turbans certainly helped to lift French women's morale during the Occupation. Their independent spirit was not easily damp-ened and wearing frivolous, individualistic fashions struck just the right note of defiance, contrasting cleverly with the conformity of their uniformed occupiers.

Fashion in Paris made great efforts not to be visually depressed by the harsh realities of the time. Designers

Above and far right: The glamorous draped dress and fabulous satin cocktail hat looked far removed from the rigours of total war affecting many parts of the world.

Right and opposite: The wartime fashions of New York had simple lines but managed to remain glamorous and sophisticated.

intensified the established silhouette; wide, padded shoulders were further emphasised with deeply-cut dolman sleeves and tightly nipped-in waists. Full, gathered, flared or drapey skirts were daringly short, barely covering the knees, and the overall silhouette of a fashion-conscious Parisian woman, from 1942 to 1944, often looked head-and foot-heavy with bath-towel-sized, draped turbans and platform-soled, wedge-heeled shoes.

Despite considerable pressure by the Nazi authorities to move the centre of couture designing to Berlin and Vienna, the French couturiers managed to stay in Paris and present small collections. Although they operated in difficult conditions, there was no shortage of customers and the French sense of style, with its sophisticated chic, couture cut and skilled workmanship still showed, and quickly regained its self-confidence and traditional ability to launch new fashion directions once Paris had been liberated in 1944. Despite the fact that the rest of the fashion world went its own way during the first half of the 40s, it marked time on major alterations to the basic silhouette until Paris was ready to launch the important changes of the early post-war years.

After the fall of France, stylish living and fashionable dressing became increasingly isolated. Technically, the citizens of neutral countries, including the US, were free to visit occupied Europe, but very few did. The fascist powers regularly denounced American culture as 'decadent' and 'racially impure' and travelling to and from Europe was difficult and potentially dangerous. Later, in 1940 and during 1941, occasional references and reports were made in the American press to French fashions and Parisian life under the German occupation. To many Americans, the France they had known was a lost world and interest in developing trends in fashion and glamour began to centre on the States, particularly New York and California.

Most of the British Empire was relatively unaffected by war until 1942, and parts of Africa and the West Indies remained so throughout the conflict, staying in a kind of time-warp, with considered occasion dressing, servants and the leisurely, colonial lifestyle of the 30s continuing in a modified form.

At home, Britain was united in resisting the enemy. Bombing, rationing and restrictions were borne with surprising cheerfulness. 'Business as usual' was the popular attitude and, although the scope for creativity was limited and shortages increased, the British fashion industry continued to operate.

English *Vogue* and *Harpers Bazaar* became smaller and thinner as the paper to print them on was restricted and stylish merchandise, worthy of featuring, more difficult to obtain. Glamorous-looking covers and lead pictures in colour were often taken from the American editions and the featured clothes were disappointingly unavailable in austerity Britain. Despite the limitations, the magazines' circulations steadily increased; well-thumbed copies were passed on and on as demand exceeded supply. Women needed the morale boost of looking at fashionable and glamorous pictures – they could still dream, even if they had few opportunities to buy high-fashion clothes.

Clothes rationing was introduced in 1941 and got progressively more severe as the War continued. Women had to plan their wardrobes with great care. Every item of clothing, apart from hats, had an allocated coupon value and choices often had to be made between basics, such as stockings and underwear, and a much-longed-for new dress or suit.

The English couture houses showed spring and autumn collections throughout the War and, although they were not able to launch new silhouettes and were subject to fabric and trimming restrictions, they managed to produce elegant, beautifully-made, individually-fitted clothes. Stylish, custom-dressed women, carefully accessorised with dressy hats and toning gloves, shoes and handbags, were still seen in fashionable stores, restaurants and hotels even at the height of the London Blitz.

Throughout the 20th century, certain cities have had their special time as the acknowledged centre of creative design and the fashionable lifestyle of the moment. Paris must hold the record for this, with high points being the *belle époque* of the 1900s and the fun-loving 20s.

New York's reputation for stylish dressing had grown steadily during the 30s; famous department stores, like Bergdorf Goodman, and Saks, were already more glamorous than their European counterparts and the wholesale fashion manufacturers of Seventh Avenue produced slick, well-cut, up to the moment designs in all price ranges, enabling New Yorkers with even modest incomes to be dressed in the latest fashion trends.

Apart from losing Paris as a source for ideas, American fashion was unaffected by the War until at least 1942 and New York became even more fashion-conscious and confident in its new role as the capital of style and glamour. Many of Paris's design talents, including Schiaparelli and Mainbocher, moved there, and Molyneux – although based in London – produced special export collections for the States, actively encouraged by the British government, anxious to earn precious US dollars to help the War effort.

The smart New York women of the early 40s had a lot going for them. Up-town New York still looked new and exciting (many of the buildings had been built in the 20s and 30s), urban violence was yet to become a problem, Broadway offered a wonderful choice of new shows and chic restaurants, and hotels and nightclubs abounded, while the stores were full of glamorous, desirable clothes.

The presentation of fashionable women was impressive and envied all over the world. American fashion, although clearly influenced by the Paris designs of 1938–40, was beginning to have a distinct and assured style of its own, with more than a hint of the kind of female power-dressing

that was later to inspire the fashions of the 1980s.

Hair was worn even longer than it had been in the late 30s and was either swept on top of the head in high pompadour rolls and curls or smoothly brushed down onto the shoulders and neatly turned under in the glamorous longer bob favoured by the female stars. Important-looking hats were tilted forward and imaginatively trimmed, or worn on the back of the head, flatteringly framing the face in a halo-shape. Day suits and dresses in classic black and navy, or clear American reds, lemon yellows, sand colours and creamy beiges had simple, well-tailored, clean-cut lines and were less fussy than European styles had been at the beginning of the War. The emphasis was on immaculate, strongly-stated accessories and a wide range of imaginative shoes and handbags were available – shiny patent leather was especially popular.

Young, style-conscious New Yorkers, shopping on crowded Fifth Avenue, showed off the new urban images of glamour in fashion. Heavy make-up was more professionally applied than ever. Foundation colour (pan-cake make up) was used to give a very smooth base for face-powder, and added clarity to eye make-up and lipstick. Mouths remained the focal point and cherry-red lips, with matching varnished finger and toenails, were very characteristic of the period. Beautifully-groomed long hair swung under halo hats, patent-leather shoulder bags hung from sharply-padded shoulders and knee-high hemlines showed off silk-stockinged legs and patent, high-heeled, sling-backed, peep-toed shoes.

Glamour had become less remote and men loved the erotic appeal of women with long, tumbling hairstyles, seamed stockings and high-heeled, strappy shoes, particularly those with ankle straps. Hollywood took full advantage of the new imagery and promoted it as an important part of the younger stars' appeal.

Rita Hayworth as a glamorous, sexy nightclub singer in

Overleaf (left): Rita Hayworth, the sex goddess of 40s films, undoubtedly starred in thousands of male fantasies.

Right: Veronica Lake's 'peek-a-boo' bob became the classic 'movie-star' hairstyle, copied by countless women on both sides of the Atlantic.

figure-clinging, draped and slit black satin, tossing her mane of long auburn hair as she teased and tempted a smouldering Glenn Ford in the well-known film, *Gilda*, must have fuelled thousands of male fantasies. She certainly made a lasting impression and became a role model of the 40s and 50s.

In the more realistic world of the 1940s, Hollywood 'Glamour Girls' were promoted more frankly for their obvious natural assets – vitality, bright good looks, attractive hair, curvy figures and well-shaped legs – rather than the carefully-cultivated, goddess-like artifice and mystique of the 30s superstars.

Betty Grable's perfect legs were nearly always shown off when she was cast as a stage dancer, with plenty of opportunity to appear in draped or frilly basques and sheer tights.

Lana Turner's young figure, in casual shorts and sweaters, caused a sensation. Clearly showing the outline of well-developed breasts in a tight-fitting sweater was still considered very revealing in the early 40s and she became famous as the original 'Sweater Girl'.

Dorothy Lamour's exotic dark-haired looks were played up by Hollywood publicity, and steamy-looking pictures of her as a South Sea Island dreamgirl in a skimpy, draped sarong, made her one of the US Army's favourite pin-up girls of the Second World War.

Latin America, a safe distance from the world's war zones, became a popular holiday destination for prosperous US citizens seeking a change of scene. It was also frequently used as a film location for colourful musicals. Latin American music had been growing in popularity since the 30s and, along with the increased interest in South America, it became even more important. Brazil's tiny but dynamic singer and dancer, Carmen Miranda, made the dazzling carnival image of Latin America world famous. She was not conventionally good-looking but her vitality and personal-ity, combined with her over-the-top outfits (turbans with enormous fruit and flower decorations, off-the-shoulder, frilled necklines, bare midriffs, and flamenco-styled skirts – slit to show off preposterously-high, platform-soled gold sandals as she danced and sang in her big production numbers) cheered wartime audiences and helped to popularise colourful Latin American influences in resortwear and evening dress.

Esther Williams, with her exciting mix of glowing, healthy good looks, curvy figure and superb proficiency as a sportswoman, helped to turn the basic swimsuit into a glamour garment. Swimwear had gradually become better-fitting and more stylish during the 30s, and aspiring young starlets were often photographed in their 'streamlined' one- and two-piece suits, but it was not until the spectacular 'acquacade' musicals of the 40s that the fashion swimsuit really came into its own. Displaying her style of graceful swimming and wearing a stunning range of designer swimwear in elasticated, printed satin, strong two-colour effects and draped and ruched lamé and iridescents, Esther Williams captured the public's imagination and made many of the young generation realise the potential of poolside glamour.

With her striking Nordic good looks inherited from her German–Danish parentage, Veronica Lake became known all over the world for her below-shoulder-length blonde hair, parted at one side and deliberately arranged to fall over one eye. The sexy Veronica Lake 'peek-a-boo' hairstyle was one of the strongest and most easy-to-achieve glamour images of the 1940s. In fact, it has become a glamour classic and one of the most copied hairstyles of the century, worn by many women in all of the following decades.

As well as bold new images for the young, there were also new role models for the more mature woman. Bette Davis, in the classic 1942 weepie *Now Voyager*, and Joan Crawford, in her 1945 award-winning role in *Mildred*

Alix's beautiful, classic, draped
evening dresses from her last
collection before the occupation
of France.

A picture hat in multi-coloured gingham, stunningly effective with a simple, dark-coloured summer suit or dress.

Pierce, both played women who, although emotionally vulnerable, became successfully competitive and self-reliant in the outside world. Their characterisations of more liberated women were reflected in their confident style presentation. Their hair was rolled up in sophisticated-looking hairstyles, heavy make-up was immaculately applied and they were power-dressed during the day in mannish, square-shouldered suits over which they wore even broader-shouldered fur coats (Joan Crawford's were memorably wide in *Mildred Pierce*). However, they managed to look meltingly feminine for off-duty evening dates in glitter-embroidered, long, softly-draped dinner dresses.

Fifty years ago, smoking was often considered smart and worldly, and rarely thought of as the anti-social health hazard it is today. Bette Davis was a great cigarette 'poser' and the scene in *Now Voyager* when Paul Henreid's character lights two cigarettes and passes one to her as tender looks are exchanged, became a hallmark of 40s togetherness.

The glamour image of men in the early and mid-40s was primarily that of men in uniform. Militarism gripped the world as never before and every kind of regime – democratic or totalitarian – glorified the fighting man. Military-trained, physically fit, well-built, strong, handsome men in smart uniforms, whether Asian, European or American, were the undisputed glamour idols of the age.

Officers' uniforms were always the most impressive and guaranteed to draw admiration from both sexes. Elitism, although less obvious than during earlier wars, was stronger than it is today and was clearly reflected in the style, cut and quality of officers' apparel. Decorated peaked caps, shoulder-widening, insignia-marked epaulettes and well-tailored tunics, belted at the waist with shiny Sam Browne leather belts and worn with trousers pressed into knife-edge creases which broke over well-buffed shoes – or tucked into short boots and ankle-covering gaiters – were worn by those in the democracies. Meanwhile, totalitarian countries admired the severe, authoritarian image of their officers' riding breeches and knee-high, polished jackboots.

The progressive mechanisation of the armed forces, particularly the growing importance of the air force, produced a new type of war hero. Fighter pilots in Britain's Royal Air Force, Germany's *Luftwaffe* and the American Air Force had to be technically proficient as well as brave. They were the new 'glory' and 'glamour' boys and hero-worshipped as the modern equivalent of the dashing cavalry officers of earlier generations.

Flying kit, particularly tough leather flying-jackets, originally designed as totally functional garments, has become a lasting fashion influence. Copies of US, leather flight jackets of the Second World War, often considered to have extra sales appeal if they are correctly-detailed reproductions, are sold all over the world and are as popular with today's young generation as they were with their fathers and grandfathers, some of whom wore the original service-issue jackets in serious combat over 50 years ago.

Film makers of the 40s got considerable mileage out of patriotic, commercially-angled war films. The physique and sex appeal of leading male heart-throbs, such as Clark Gable, Errol Flynn and Robert Taylor, were heightened by presenting them as smart, uniformed, naval, army, and airforce officers. Some of the stars were so successful in their military roles that they were cast as officers in each of the services several times over within a couple of years. Although they always played brave men, in the new realism of the war years they sometimes appeared unshaven, sweaty and battle-weary. Even 'stiff-upper-lipped' British war films, featuring cool, courageous RAF pilots with their Edwardian dandy handlebar moustaches and nonchalantly-tied silk scarves, showed the growing stress felt by air crews subjected to successive flying missions over enemy territory.

As a welcome contrast to the War, actors were still cast

in civilian roles. Raymond-Chandler-type detectives or undercover agents, played with rough-diamond charm by Spencer Tracy or Humphrey Bogart, were especially popular and the clothes worn by them in these American films had an unexpected influence on men's fashion. Gentlemanly elegance was less admired in the tougher atmosphere of the decade and the easy, confident swagger of American-style, wide-brim fedora pull-on hats and loose-fitting, broadly-padded suits and coats caught the mood of the time.

The great outdoors of the Americas and the Pacific islands were popular peacetime settings for escapist movies. Tropical islands, particularly Hawaii (far less commercial-ised in the early 40s than it is today), provided the perfect background for colourful, musical romances in which macho stars, like Burt Lancaster and Victor Mature, dressed in bright, Hawaiian-print shirts and shorts, chased after a hard-to-get Betty Grable or Dorothy Lamour. These lighthearted films helped to popularise more adventurous casual-wear for men and brightly-printed shirts, shorts and ties became an established part of American menswear during the 40s. They were later successfully revived as an international fashion trend of the 1980s.

Romance on the beaches also helped to promote boxer-style swim shorts. Men's swimwear, like women's, had improved during the 30s and the basic one-piece vest-like suit, so unflattering to most men, had gradually been replaced by swimming shorts. These had become noticeably more modern-looking by the 40s and, at a time when it was still not acceptable to show the unclothed male body on the screen, showing off the athletic-looking, tanned torsos of young male stars in their swimming trunks was permitted. It boosted their sex appeal with cinema audiences and helped to launch 'beach boy' body-culture which was to become such an important feature of male glamour in later decades.

John Wayne and Alan Ladd, riding the range in

Western shirts, well-worn jeans and cowboy boots, were the first of many stars who portrayed the strong, macho image of self-reliant men in America's frontier days. The image appealed to the instincts of bravado in many men and inspired the ever-popular cult of the urban- and suburban-cowboy.

The influence of the American teenager continued to grow and, although rather basic and homely by later standards, adolescents already had their own style of dressing. Girls and boys hung out at their local café or dancehall in 'sloppy joe' sweaters, rolled-up jeans and sneakers or gym shoes. They idolised the world-famous 'swing bands' of Glenn Miller, Benny Goodman and Tommy Dorsey, and identified with some of the up-and-coming lead singers – particularly the young Frank Sinatra – who looked skinny and vulnerably adolescent in slightly oversized suits. When he sang 'Nancy With the Laughing Face', teenage bobby-soxers screamed their appreciation and girls squealed with emotion and fainted. The media revelled in the new sensation and it was clear that the age of the young male pop star, that was to transform glamour images for men, had dawned.

America emerged from the Second World War as the most powerful nation in the world and, like dominant nations throughout the centuries, it had its prosperous way of life copied and used as a standard by other countries. Although America hadn't produced dramatic or obviously revolutionary changes in fashion or glamour, the internationally-admired ideal had acquired an American accent, and the USA took the lead in contemporary ways of dressing.

The glamour image for women was curvier, more womanly and less dauntingly willowy and snake-hipped than it had been in the sophisticated 30s. The mid-40s was one of the few periods in the century when the bust, waist, hips and legs were given equal importance. Breasts were pushed out and upwards in their uplift bras, waists were

Chic outfits and a wide choice of fashionable shoes were available for American women to wear to the British War Relief Cocktail Matinee.

Glamour retained – upswept hair and a British wartime 'two-piece', a flared peplum and narrow skirt.

Above and left: Lauren Bacall showed two contrasting American fashion images – the 'power-dressed' sharp suit and the meltingly-feminine evening dress.

shaped and fitted – but not yet contorted in – and attractively-curved hips were emphasised with peplum jackets and draped skirts. Hemlines were still placed just below the knee, making well-shaped legs almost as important as they had been in the 20s, and the whole basis for looking good in the fashions of the period depended on having a well-proportioned figure with all the classic curves in the right places.

In contrast to the high-gloss image of smart New Yorkers and Hollywood 'Glamour Girls', the developing, easy-going, comfortable and more mobile American way of life began to affect the way many women dressed. The labour-saving home, complete with laundry, barbecue and swimming pool, plus the essential car (sometimes two or more per family) for easy access to shopping centres, sports facilities, schools and university campuses, so familiar all over the world today, was already becoming established in the States in the 1940s.

The social changes were reflected in a much more casual approach to everyday clothes. Urban-looking day and afternoon dresses, tailored spring and autumn coats and suits worn with a range of appropriate hats, which had been the basis of women's wardrobes for several decades, now looked too formal and dressed-up and began to be confined more and more to big-city and special-occasion dressing.

Many women went hatless and the more naturally-glamorous head, with well-cut, manageable hair, whether long or short, began to replace the more complicated rolled and pinned-up styles that had been fashionable for so long.

Pretty, feminine-looking dresses were more simply-styled and easy-to-wear, with fitted or shirt-style bodices and pleated, gathered or flared skirts. Endlessly-useful, interchangeable separates, jackets (sometimes with attachable hoods for winter), knitwear, blouses, skirts and trousers, accessorised with headscarves, roomy shoulderbags and low- or wedge-heeled shoes, formed the basic range of clothes that suited the post-war woman's changing way of life.

Glamour for many younger women began to have more to do with natural, healthy-looking good looks and well-shaped bodies, shown off in casual-wear, rather than the more contrived, artificial and ladylike images of their mothers' generation.

Europe had been so badly devastated and impoverished by the Second World War that many people in 1945 felt it could never hope to regain its former position as the centre for the decorative arts, stylish living and luxurious clothes, or be the leader of new directions in fashion. Eastern Europe had been absorbed into the Russian communist empire, German cities and industries lay in ruins, and many countries – including Britain – were turning to socialism and a more egalitarian way of life. Young fashion designers of the time were often advised to leave Europe and take their talents to the more receptive fashion markets of New York, California and Hollywood.

Despite the all-pervading atmosphere of austerity, with power cuts and acute shortages of all commodities, including fabrics, the Paris couturiers presented their first peacetime collections in 1945. The press and the all-important American buyers not only found the collections full of inventive and potentially commercial ideas, they also saw the first confident signs of a change to the long-established basic silhouette.

The new fashions reminded the world that Paris design had not lost its tradition of femininity, chic and glamour. The early post-war fashions seemed to express women's longing for escape from the harsh realities of the day and regress into the more secure, pre-1914 world of elegant living. Nostalgia was a recurring theme in all the collections.

Hair was smoothly brushed back into a chignon on the crown of the head or the nape of the neck. Hats lost the inflated look of the occupation years and were often pillbox or boater shapes, less heavily-trimmed and worn on top of

the head or tilted-back, to show the smoother hairlines.

Shoulders were rounded and noticeably less padded, while bodices were more fitted over the breasts and nipped into the waist with clever darting and pulled-in belts. Suit jackets followed the same line and lost the mannish, hard, tailored look of the early 40s. Skirts were either narrow and figure-hugging or full and flared, with hemlines lengthening each season. By the autumn of 1946, most couturiers were showing upper-calf-length for day-wear and mid- and lower-calf for late day and evening.

Spanish-born Christobal Balenciaga, who became one of the most important designers of the late 40s and the 1950s, moved to Paris during the Spanish Civil War and quickly became recognised as one of the most interesting designers of the late 30s. He helped to pioneer the feminising of fashion in the early post-war years, showing fuller and longer skirts as early as the spring of 1945, and soon acquired his well-respected reputation for being several years ahead of most designers in the evolution of new fashion trends.

Jacques Fath was one of the most commercially successful young designers of the 40s who, like Balenciaga, became noticed just before the War. He managed to continue to build up his name during the occupation and quickly expanded his business once the War was over. His style of designing was sharp and bright, always very feminine and based on a close, curvy fit and he liked to lighten up suits, blouses and dresses with crisp white collars and cuffs and trim his tailored coats and suits with contrasting-coloured fur collars – black Persian lamb on emerald green, or white ermine on inky blue. Day dresses in neat checks or brightly-coloured plain fabrics were tightly belted at the waist with wide, patent leather belts and full

Top left: Constance Bennett's classy, urban 'high-society' look – matching pearl jewellery and pompadour hairdo, topped with flowers.

Paris couture during the German occupation still produced surprisingly extravagant styles and presented small collections, despite the difficult conditions.

skirts fanned out in sun-ray pleats. The strong visual impact of his clothes was popular with private clients like Rita Hayworth and Eva Peron, who found that his clothes enhanced their glamorous images. His designing also appealed to American wholesale manufacturers anxious to adapt his eye-catching styles for the ready-to-wear market.

Pierre Balmain was another talented designer who helped to re-establish international interest in the Paris couture. He loved to glamorise women; Jolie Madame became his trademark and his 'pretty woman' philosophy remained constant whatever direction fashion decided to take. In his early collections he was greatly influenced by the fashions of the early 1910s. He revived long, flared-out tunics worn over very narrow slit skirts, and peg-top and hip-draped effects tapering into tight hemlines. His figure-moulding, strapless satin evening dresses with their long,

Above: Whenever possible, the many young women serving in the armed forces retained their glamour looks.

American 'pin-up' glamour, emphasising womanly curves, cheered up thousands of men in the armed forces.

expertly-draped hobble skirts, glittering jewellery and shoulders wrapped in deep fox stoles represented an almost fairytale glamour to Europe's many struggling Cinderellas of the mid-40s.

In February 1947, America was well on the way to post-war prosperity and expansion. American store buyers and Seventh Avenue manufacturers were happy to have Paris back as a source of new ideas which they could adapt to suit Stateside tastes. The smart departmental stores were displaying their early spring merchandise which showed Parisian influences with softer shoulder-lines and longer skirts.

However, post-war recovery still seemed a long way off in Europe and rationing, shortages and endless restrictions made everyday life a hard slog for most people. To make matters worse, Europe was in the grip of one of the most severe winters ever known – in Germany and Eastern Europe many people died of hypothermia. It could not have seemed a worse moment to launch some of the most extravagant fashions of the century, but mild-mannered Christian Dior, putting the final touches to his first collection in the Avenue Montaigne in Paris, was about to do just that.

Above: The 1990 film *Memphis Belle* successfully recreated the look of the wartime fighter pilot – the kit became a lasting influence.

Above: Vivien Leigh's timeless beauty and sex appeal were enhanced by her romantic-looking neo-Victorian balldress.

Above (right): The mature and handsome Cary Grant starred alongside the beautiful and chic Ingrid Bergman in the 1946 spy-thriller *Notorious*.

Right: Robert Mitchum's classic 'tough-guy' image, complete with fedora hat and trenchcoat.

Above: Adele Simpson's Profile dress anticipated the 'New Look'.

Joan Crawford achieved her woman-of-the-world look with immaculate make-up, rolled-up hair, simple, chic dress, eye-catching jewellery and sling-backed court shoes.

The Post-War Revival

The Late 40s to the Mid-50s

Halfway through the first showing of Christian Dior's now legendary 'New Look', as his models confidently swirled in and out of the elegant showrooms, brushing the audience and high-standing ashtrays with their long, extravagantly-full skirts, attentively watching women pulled at their own skirts as if they felt they were too short and skimpy. Dior's timing was perfect. After years of war and austerity women longed to wear glamorous, ultra-feminine clothes.

Opposite: Christian Dior's flattering pale-pink outfit epitomised his interpretation of glamour — accentuated femininity and romantic elegance.

The 'New Look' was not quite as new as the media hype of 1947 proclaimed. The trend towards very feminine, body-fitting clothes, influenced by the Victorian and Edwardian eras, had grown through the 30s and was the dominant theme of the Paris collections of 1938 and '39. The War postponed their development but soon after the Paris designers tentatively took up where they had left off and softened and feminised fashion a little more each season. Their most extravagant designs for autumn 1946 were very similar to the least extreme versions of Dior's spring 1947 'New Look'.

Christian Dior expounded and exaggerated the developing fashions further than most people would have dared contemplate in the atmosphere of the time, and in doing so earned himself a prominent place in the history of fashion.

Many women, particularly in Europe, had not been able to follow the trends that foreshadowed the 'New Look', and felt that Dior's total top-to-toe concept had outdated their entire wardrobe in a single season.

The 'New Look' started at the top with hair that was brushed back into a chignon or swept and rolled to one side. Hats were smaller, softer-looking, draped pill-boxes worn on the side of the head and lightly trimmed with feathers, or Edwardian boater-shapes tilted back off the face and delicately swathed with veiling.

Shoulders were very sloped and, to emphasise the downward line, sleeves were sometimes cut full under the armhole in a dolman shape – they narrowly fitted the arms and were often worn with long, slightly ruched gloves. Breasts were exaggerated and pushed out further than nature had ever intended, bodices fitted like second skins and waists were pulled in to Victorian wasp-waists. Hips were padded out and further highlighted by short, fluted jackets and immensely-full, flared skirts (as much as 25 yards of material were used in one skirt). Day-length varied from bottom-of-the-calf to just-above-the-ankle.

Left: Dior's 1947 'New Look' exaggerated the developing fashion trends further than most people would have thought possible and outdated women's wardrobes in a single season.

Stockings were a smoky-grey beige colour and shoes were plain, high-heeled court shoes or finely-strapped-round-the-ankle styles.

The 'New Look' was probably the most sensational and controversial fashion launch of the century. Predictably, goverments grappling with severe shortages and embarking on the mammoth task of reconstruction condemned the new fashions and appealed to women to boycott them for patriotic reasons. Britain even seriously considered prohibiting their production.

It was all to no avail. Women wanted to wear the 'New Look' as soon as possible. American manufacturers rushed commercial adaptations into their stores within weeks in a blaze of publicity. Other parts of the world, despite rationing and restrictions, followed as quickly as they could and, although the 'New Look' in its most extreme form was rarely worn and didn't last, its influence endured and was far-reaching, continuing well into the 50s.

The decade from the late 1940s to the late 50s was the last period when the leading couture designers' influence was so strong that it verged on the dictatorial. The post-Second-World-War era was a stark contrast to the frivolous 20s; purposeful reconstruction in a divided world took place against the backdrop of the Iron Curtain and the Cold War. Conformity, even in following fashion, characterised the times. Dior and Balenciaga were the most important couturiers and their collections made front page news, with any alterations in silhouettes and skirt-lengths reported as if they were world-shaking events.

Dior's style of designing was always based on shapes constructed to show off womanly curves. He revived – in a modified form – the pre-1914 concept of helping to give women the required shape as a pre-requisite to wearing fashionable clothes. His dresses often had their own built-in bras, lightly-corsetted waists and stitched-in petticoats. Fine, lightweight fabrics were frequently mounted on

Above: The influence of the 'New Look' clearly seen in Jacques Fath's tightly-fitted topcoat and dressy, full-skirted suit.

The height of late 40s sophistication.

firmer materials to give dresses the contrived shape of the season. Even his suit jackets were darted into taped waistlines and canvassed to stand away from the hips. Evening dresses were sometimes so heavily constructed that they could stand on their own, waiting for the wearer to step into them.

After the non-fit of the 20s, the body-cling of the 30s and the mannish tailoring of the early 40s, many women welcomed a more confining fit in clothes that did something for their figures and had glamour and sex appeal. Despite greater complications in production, garment manufacturers adapted Dior's designs as basic lines for the mass market. Men settling back into civilian life appreciated their women's curvy fashions; the post-war birth rate soared and today, older men nostalgically recall the decade when accentuating the female form was all-important and 'women looked like women'.

Dior designed with taste and elegance. His clothes were beautifully-proportioned, with great care taken over the size of collars, revers and pockets, the placing of buttons and the use of trimmings. He kept embroidery and decoration mainly for cocktail and evening dresses and relied on his fashion shapes – made in high-quality fine wools, wool and silk mixtures, smooth-face cloths and silk-lined tweeds – to give his day clothes their stylish impact. He made great use of discreet, classic colourings, favouring all shades of grey, sophisticated black, navy and creamy beiges for his spring collections. Dior livened up his shows with unexpected splashes of bright primary colours – a brilliant-red topcoat, a clear-blue day-dress, or an emerald-green city suit.

The designer's love for the romantic elegance of the 19th century was most clearly reflected in his evening dresses. He popularised designs with plunging necklines, tightly-moulded bodices and very full, lower-calf-length, ballet-style skirts, made in fine, corded silk, lightweight taffeta and satins with a subtle sheen. Colours were flattering – pale ice-pink, oyster shades, soft lilacs, mauves, blue-greys and black. Dresses often had their own matching stoles, which were sometimes lined with a contrasting colour, pink with pale grey or an oyster shade with black.

Dior's interpretation of glamour was to accentuate femininity. Women at parties and receptions, filling rooms with their tiny-waisted, crinoline-style dresses and shoulders elegantly draped in stoles, looked pretty and appealing in a way that had not been fashionable since the turn of the century.

Christian Dior died in 1957 after ten years of fame and international recognition that made his name one of the most established in the fashion world. His contribution to 20th-century fashion has often been debated and compared to that of other famous designers. His concept didn't have the originality or endurance of Balenciaga's, nor did it have the recurring influence of Chanel, but he helped women to feel good about the way they looked in clothes that showed them off as the most feminine of females. His designs cheered up sombre, difficult times and he did much to re-establish Paris as the most creative and influential fashion centre in the world.

Although Balenciaga was never as well-known with the general public as Dior, his design concept was a major influence for nearly 20 years. He had been at the forefront of the trend for very fitted clothes; his designs, however, were not as romantically pretty as Dior's. They had a more sculptured, slightly architectural quality, which he began to develop more noticeably in the early 1950s when he introduced his semi-fitted look.

Clothes that were not shaped tightly to the curves of the figure were a radical departure for the time. Balenciaga first used his new line for suits and coats. They were still very constructed, interlined and often mounted on canvas, but the shape was sculptured to shadow the curves of the breasts and waist rather than fit them; some designs had semi-fitted

Pierre Balmain loved to glamorise
women. His *jolie madame*
philosophy is well-illustrated by two
designs of the early 50s – his hour-
glass suit (right) and sumptuous
balldress (above).

fronts and loose backs cut to fold under like a cape – it was a particularly elegant line for calf-length topcoats. To complete his styles, Balenciaga set collars away from the base of the neck and soon became known for his new standaway necklines.

His model girls, who were striking rather than conventionally beautiful or pretty, wore their hair pinned back in French pleats, and completed their outfits with small, very simple pill-box or saucer-shaped hats worn straight across the forehead.

His very individual line, with its precisely-groomed heads, long, unadorned necks, round rather than sloped shoulders, subtly-shaped, perfectly-balanced, hip-length jackets and pencil-slim, mid-calf-length skirts, was a very elegant – almost austere – understated style, where the exact placing of a button or the subtle proportioning of a collar was the all-important feature of the design. It was the first really original fashion concept to be born after the Second World War.

Some women, accustomed to the femininity of earlier fashions, initially found Balenciaga's style too severe. The fashion world, however, admired his new idea and it became the high fashion ideal of the late 50s. Designers in London and New York, as well as Paris, followed his lead and began moving away from figure-accentuating lines for day clothes.

Givenchy and Courreges, later to become famous in their own right, were early disciples of Balenciaga's style. This was clearly shown in Givenchy's successful designs for Audrey Hepburn. The Balenciaga influence was seen even in the star's early films – *Sabrina Fair*, made in 1954, and particularly in the fashion-orientated *Funny Face* in 1957. Hepburn's wistful, gamine looks were transformed in both films from a dowdy student image to high-fashion chic. Many of the young who had grown up after the War identified with Audrey Hepburn; her looks and slim figure were perfect for showing off the new fashion directions and she helped to popularise a less obvious kind of young glamour.

By the mid-50s, Balenciaga was developing his semi-fitted look for dresses as well as tailored garments. He showed lightly-shaped, long tunics over very narrow skirts and the same line for easy-fitting dresses. He also shortened his hemlines to the top of the calf (the shortest length for ten years). The press talked about 'a return to the skimpy shapeless 20s'. In fact, his new chemise line *was* shaped; dresses were skilfully cut to indicate the bust and waist, outline the hips and taper into a constricting hemline. It was a subtle, attractive line, shadowing the figure and emphasising a long, leggy look. Semi-fitted suits and slender chemise dresses, shortened to just below the knee, became the basic silhouettes of the late 50s and Balenciaga's influence reigned supreme for several years.

Easy-fitting shapes, with ever-shortening hemlines, continued well into the next decade but, as designing became wilder and more anti-establishment, Balenciaga's disciplined elegance no longer appealed to the young trendsetters of the 60s and it became associated with the fashion image of well-dressed, older women.

Top fashion artists in the 20s and 30s not only illustrated the latest fashions superbly, they were also talented enough to be able to draw appropriate backgrounds. Eric's drawings for *Vogue* were some of the best, conveying the ultimate in stylishness. Enviably tall, slender, ultra-chic women were shown on balconies overlooking exclusive resorts, in smart restaurants with distinguished-looking male escorts or in animated conversation with an equally well-dressed girlfriend. They were drawn at fashionable race meetings, wearing stunning evening dresses in stately ballrooms, or dancing at jazzy nightclubs. Women admired and were influenced by the imagery of these fashion drawings and it was a great compliment to be described as 'looking like a fashion plate'.

Overleaf: Draped satin pillbox hats, glittering earrings, furs and long gloves were all important features of cocktail and informal evening wear.

The importance of fashion photography had grown steadily during the 30s and Horst and Cecil Beaton were already well-known for the artistry of their pictures by the early 40s. After the Second World War, fashion photography really came into its own and added another dimension to the portrayal of glamour in fashion.

The 50s were vintage years; creative photographers with a great sense of style and elegance – Irving Penn, Richard Avendon, Helmut Newton, Richard Dormer and Norman Parkinson – worked with a generation of exceptional-looking, photogenic model girls. The Latin archetype, Bettina, and Alla's look of the Orient (she was one of Dior's favourite models), America's gorgeous redhead, Suzie Parker, and the British thoroughbreds – Barbara Goalan, Fiona Campbell-Walter, Ann Gunning and Wenda Rogerson (who was married to Norman Parkinson) – were all perfect for showing off the couturiers' high-fashion looks and lines.

Immaculately-dressed models in figure-sculpting suits, sweeping coats and bouffant-skirted dresses were pictured less statically, and were often photographed on location: in the buzz of Manhattan streets, the elegance of London St James's, or against romantic-looking backgrounds in Paris and Rome. As well as presenting the strong fashion silhouettes, the pictures caught a mood and had drama and personality. They were more 'alive' and easy to relate to than fashion drawings – almost like shots from movies. The photographers were the directors and the models their stars, who became known all over the world; some joined the international jet set and married rich, powerful men, and famous model girls' looks, make-up, hairstyles and mannerisms were copied by young fashion-conscious women everywhere. Like film stars, models had become 20th-century idols.

Hollywood's influence on glamour and fashion was still strong, but not quite as powerful as it had been in the 30s

and early 40s. Extensive press coverage following the success of Dior's 'New Look' made the dictates of the new leading designers and fashion photography all-important; the novelty of television and the growing interest in making homes more comfortable and better equipped began to affect lifestyles and cinema audiences started to decline.

The new post-war female stars were some of the most beautiful and memorable in movie history and were admired almost as much for their curvy figures as for their facial good looks.

The young Elizabeth Taylor, with her breathtakingly beautiful eyes and perfect features, showed off her shapely figure and managed to be youthfully slender and yet

The young Elizabeth Taylor and moody Montgomery Clift made a beautiful couple in the intensely romantic film, *A Place in the Sun.*

curvaceous in very feminine dresses, which were designed to emphasise full breasts with skilful drapery, lace inserts and plunging necklines. The pretty, busty dresses, with nipped-in waists and full skirts, which she wore in *A Place in the Sun* (where she played a rich girl involved in a desperately intense romance with a poor, tentative and nervous Montgomery Clift), and her slightly more mature-looking bust- and hip-clinging dresses in *Cat on a Hot Tin Roof* (where she sets out to make herself irresistible to a rather sullen Paul Newman), helped to make her one of the most admired sex symbols of the 50s.

Ava Gardner also had a sensational face and figure; her sultry, sensual, womanly looks appealed to many nationali-

Ava Gardner's sultry, sensual, womanly good looks had worldwide appeal.

ties and she was especially popular with the Latin countries of Europe and South America.

So much has already been said and written about Marilyn Monroe – her looks, figure and personality, with its endearing mixture of innocence, frank sexiness and vulnerability, were captivating. She is as well-known today, 30 years after her death, as she was at the height of her career. Countless women have been influenced by her style; model girls commercialised it, 70s pop star Blondie (Debbie Harry) adapted it, and megastar Madonna has made it an integral part of her look since the mid-80s. Marilyn was more than a superstar role model – she became the most famous female glamour image of the 20th century.

For all her starriness and her famous hip-wiggling walk, Marilyn had a kind of ordinariness in her presentation, which appealed to the more casual attitudes of the 50s. Her appearance was not as contrived and formally dressed-up as earlier Hollywood stars; she rarely wore hats and, although her wavy, blonde hairstyles and medium-length bobs were widely copied, they were more naturally arranged and never had a 'straight from the hairdresser' look.

Her long, sexy, figure-hugging, glittering sheath dresses were kept for big production numbers including musicals like *Gentlemen Prefer Blondes* and *There's No Business Like Show Business*. Generally, both on and off screen, she wore mainstream young women's fashions of the day and was often pictured in casual shirts, sweaters and tapered pants or jeans. Her neat, fitted suits and girly, clinging dresses (including the immortalised white dress which billowed up so effectively in *The Seven Year Itch*), worn with strappy, high-heeled shoes, could have come from a middle-of-the-range department store rather than a Hollywood design studio. It was part of her success – she was unique, but the Monroe image was less remote; it was one women could identify with, and men hoped to meet women with the 'Marilyn Monroe Look'.

Left and top right: The clever use of colour and fabric gave added interest to the established evening-dress silhouette.

Bottom right: Jacques Fath's charmingly pretty afternoon dresses captured the appeal of the ultra-feminine mid-century fashions.

The 50s was probably the last decade in which Grace Kelly's cool, classy, ladylike style had a wide enough appeal to make her an international superstar. The 'Grace Kelly Look' was more New York and London than Paris or Hollywood. She avoided strong, couture designer lines and starry outfits with exaggerated figure show. Her blonde hair was pulled back into a neat chignon or French pleat, or arranged in a flattering medium-length bob. Her city outfits were always accessoried with appropriate hats, shoes, gloves and handbags. She wore classic, 50s-style, fitted topcoats, suits with slim rather than moulded skirts, and elegantly-feminine, full-skirted dresses. Her glamour image really came into its own with her formal evening dresses and she looked stunningly beautiful with her hair swept off her face, showing off expensive earrings and necklaces, and her ball-dresses with strapless, embroidered bodices, matching stoles and sweepingly-full skirts made her look almost regal. In retrospect it was as if she was rehearsing for her future 'real life' role as Princess Grace of Monaco.

Glamour images in the first post-war decade combined influences from the leading Paris designers, famous model girls and the new generation of film stars.

Hairstyling was more natural-looking and various lengths were fashionable; short, wavy and softly-curled hair (the 'bubble cut') and styles cut to follow the shape of the head, feathered onto the cheeks and into a wind-ruffled fringe (Audrey Hepburn's 'urchin cut', with its irregular fringe, was greatly copied) were all popular alternatives to page-boy bobs (which were generally shorter than the shoulder-hanging lengths of the 40s). Pony-tails springing out from the crown of the head, often worn with hoop earrings, soon became a 50s teenage classic and, like the bob, were revised and updated in all of the following decades.

After 20 years of emphasised mouths, the make-up accent shifted to the eyes; natural eyebrows were thickened, lids shaded and the corners of the eyes pencilled to slope slightly upwards in the 'doe-eyed look'. Lips were less aggressively red and softer, pink-tinted shades became fashionable. Later in the 50s, as eye make-up intensified, lips paled even further and chalky-pink lipsticks, such as 'young pink', became a craze with girls in their teens and early 20s.

Figure-accentuating fashions were a gift to Hollywood, and the curvaceous figure, with particular emphasis on large breasts, was an essential part of overt glamour looks. A prominent bust as a focus of sex appeal, particularly in America, was a great characteristic of the early and mid-50s, and Jane Russell and Jayne Mansfield topped the league of curvaceous beauties who set a dauntingly high standard of development. Women who were not well-endowed had never felt so disadvantaged and padded or blown-up 'falsies' were frequently worn, despite the potential embarrassment of them being discovered.

Later in the 50s, although resisted at first by Hollywood image-makers, figure emphasis began to decline. Skirts shortened, stiletto-heeled, pointed shoes became popular and fashion started to concentrate on legs and feet more strongly than at any time since the 20s.

The 50s was a 'half-way house' decade that looked back to earlier, traditional values and forward to new concepts. This was well-illustrated in women's fashions but it was also reflected in men's clothes and glamour images.

Post-war men, anxious to enjoy the comforts of the home again, initially returned to the conformist stereotype of the reliable guardian of family life. They wore conventional suits, shirts and ties, longish raincoats and topcoats, along with hats, gloves and classic lace-up shoes. Tailoring was easier-fitting and formality had lessened, but the basic pre-war concept had hardly changed.

British men delved even further back for style inspiration, to the imperial past and revived, turn-of-the-century, Edwardian fashions. Tall, classic, British officer-type looks suited the style perfectly, with high-fastening jackets shaped like elegant riding jackets, worn over fancy-patterned silk waistcoats teamed with narrow, stove-piped trousers and accessoried with curved-brim bowler hats tilted forward, and long, rolled umbrellas hooked over the arm. The style – which started out as such an upper-class image – was copied and characterised by Britain's new generation of affluent, young, working-class men, and the Edwardian dandy went downmarket and was soon renamed the 'teddy boy'.

At first, film-makers seemed at a loss in finding new male glamour images and continued with variations on well-established themes. Manly roles – war heroes, cowboys, period-costume adventurers, detectives and undercover agents – were all considered solidly commercial.

The impeccably-tailored leading gentleman, utterly reliable under a flippant exterior, who had been so admired in the 30s, was considered very out-of-date by the 50s. An exception was Cary Grant, who many women found even more attractive as he grew older. His good physique, greying-at-the-temples, handsome, mature looks and his suave, man-of-the-world charm, in films such as *To Catch a Thief* – where he co-starred with Grace Kelly – helped to make him the 50s ideal of the smooth, sophisticated older man.

Many young men, who grew up after the War, rejected the conformity and complacency of the 1950s and looked for new idols and role models to identify with and admire. They found them in the new generation of film actors.

France's Gerard Philipe, Britain's Dirk Bogarde, and especially America's Montgomery Clift, Marlon Brando and James Dean, all conveyed very different ideas on looks, style and behaviour. Their attitudes were sensitive, vulnerable, vaguely anti-establishment and sometimes potentially violent. Their moody good looks were less groomed and glossy than those of previous stars. Hair was worn in a crew cut or quiffed with longer sideboards and was sometimes greased back into a duck's tail effect, and leather jackets over roll-neck sweaters were preferred to suits with shirts and ties.

Grace Kelly, cool, classy and assured, alongside Cary Grant – the attractive, older, suave man-of-the-world.

James Dean (far left) and Marlon Brando (above) popularised the macho appeal of leather biker jackets, boots and Levi jeans, which has remained constant for four decades.

The macho images of Marlon Brando in *The Wild One* and James Dean in *Rebel Without A Cause*, wearing leather motorbike jackets, T-shirts and classic Levi jeans over biker boots, had instant appeal and have become one of the most-copied young men's looks of the last 40 years. Each decade presented its own up-dated version of the look. In the 60s, longer hair had a 'Beatle fringe', the leather jacket was cut smaller and tighter jeans were worn over chisel-toed Chelsea boots. Early-70s hair straggled over the shoulders, Mexican-bandit moustaches drooped, skinny-fitting leather jackets were worn over even skinnier tank-tops and flared jeans flapped over high-heeled, platform-soled boots. By the 80s, hair was shorter and neater, heavily-detailed leather jackets blousoned out, jeans straightened over cowboy boots, and the 90s began with the original 50s image back in fashion, complete with greased-back hair, Levi 501 jeans and classic, leather biker jackets and boots.

Apart from establishing the classless, streetwise credibility of leather jackets and jeans, the 50s also saw the beginning of young, gang-style dressing. Bikers (or 'ton-up kids') in their leather gear, were one of the first and most enduring of the later 20th-century-style cults. The gang of boys tearing around on bikes, sometimes with girlfriends riding pillion, and dressed in black leather jackets and trousers, gauntlet gloves and boots, was an obvious outlet for young male aggression and an opportunity to present a rather menacing, raw kind of sexy glamour. In the 60s and 70s, this uninhibited, blatantly sexy image was developed even further by many of the successful pop stars.

In contrast to anti-establishment trends, new versions of more traditional men's looks and clothes had begun to emerge by the mid-50s. Pull-on hats and big-shouldered, loosely-draped jackets and topcoats, worn with easy-fitting, front-pleated trousers, had been the basic line for so long that fathers and sons in the first half of the 50s didn't have the usual generation gap in following fashion, and often wore the same kind of outfits. However, this began to change as the career-orientated members of the new, independently-minded generation looked for their own sharp, urban style.

Italy – with its inherent sense of taste and panache – built up its reputation as a fashion centre during the 50s and was in the forefront of new style directions for men. Italian designers introduced a different cut, a much more pared-down silhouette with natural, slightly-extended shoulder lines and narrower fitting but shorter-length jackets, slim ties and tapered trousers without pleats, worn over high-fastening, pointed-toed shoes or ankle boots.

It was a leaner, younger look, uncluttered and 50s-modern, best shown off on slim, boyish physiques and complemented by and related to Balenciaga's leggy, easy-fitting line for women. The influence of the Italian look continued into the 60s when it became the basic silhouette for style-conscious men's clothes and established Milan as the leading city for menswear design.

Social change and fashion became more lighthearted and youth-orientated in the second half of the 50s. A more serious atmosphere had prevailed in the earlier part of the decade, particularly in Europe on the frontier of the East-West divide, with the ever-present threat that the Cold War might turn atomic-bomb-hot. Uncertainty, as always, made people turn to escapism and the nostalgia of more glamorous times. Pre-war-style social life was revived in a modified form. In Britain, despite a prolonged period of austerity and high taxation, dressed-up social occasions and the famous 'London season' were successfully reinstated.

The London couturiers (the 'Top Twelve') designed with the special events of the social season very much in mind and English *Vogue* and *Harpers Bazaar* always produced pages in their early summer issues on the correct choice of clothes. A figure-fitting silk suit or a full- or draped-skirted afternoon dress in a discreet print, worn under a plain navy, tent-shaped duster coat with a smart but unexaggerated hat was recommended for the opening of the Royal Academy Art Exhibition. Dressier, longer, fuller-skirted outfits (although not the pre-war ankle-length) with more striking, wide-brimmed 'East to West' hats were suggested for Ascot and garden parties. Slim, tailored, linen or jersey suits, or sleeveless sheath dresses with matching jackets, and simple, saucer-shaped hats were considered right for spectating at Wimbledon; and outfits that were less fussy than Ascot but more dressed-up than Wimbledon were advised for the Henley Regatta. In 1953, however, English *Vogue* cautioned its readers, 'The Henley Regatta where men steal the scene calls for light colours which don't compete with the brilliance of their blazers.'

The London designers never tried to set controversial new lines and looks – they didn't have the authority that Paris held. Rarefied French chic, which put clothes on a higher plane than styles that were just in the latest fashion, or the immaculate high-gloss of smart New Yorkers, although admired objectively, didn't really appeal to most English women and perhaps didn't look as good in British settings; elegance and prettiness were preferred and well-provided by London's couturiers.

Digby Morton, Charles Creed and Michael were known for the understated British elegance of their tailoring and Norman Hartnell and Victor Steibel were lauded for their evening dresses. Mattli, Hardy Amies and John Cavanagh designed with more cosmopolitan dash, and Cavanagh's years spent with Molyneux showed in his designs – they had a lighter, more feminine, less typically-British quality.

Debutante dances with the opportunity to meet suitable young men were the highpoints of the season for the year's young debs, and their ball-dresses had to be romantically pretty in a fairytale way. Always in pale colours, they had tightly-moulded bodices, bare or softly-veiled shoulders and very full, floor-sweeping, crinoline-style skirts. White was very popular and traditionally worn for Queen Charlotte's

Ball, one of the most publicised events of the season.

Categorised and conventionally appropriate styles of dressing were still considered important and were carefully followed by the middle and upper classes well into the 50s. All this, however, was about to change and some of the most dramatic transformations came from Britain's younger generation.

The 15 years from 1939 to 1954 was the longest period in the century when clothes with the Chanel label were not available. Why Coco Chanel closed her couture business for so long, and then reopened it at the age of 70 has never been fully explained, although many theories have been advanced.

She was reputed to have been sympathetic to the Nazis and to have left France at the end of the War and taken up residence in Switzerland to avoid investigation, even though she had kept her fashion house closed during the occupation, when their was money to be made and many of her contemporaries continued to produce twice-yearly collections.

Declining interest in Chanel's famous perfumes as her image as a contemporary designer faded and became associated with an earlier generation, might well have been the most compelling reason for her to re-enter couture designing.

Quotes from Chanel reflect her hostile attitude to the fashions of the late 40s and early 50s, ridiculing their exaggerated fit and constructed shapes as retrograde and unsuited to the modern world. This was despite the fact that she had gone along with the ever more figure-conscious lines of the 30s, and had featured tight, strapless bodices and nipped-in waists in her last pre-war collections.

In an interview just before her comeback in 1954, she declared herself ready to do battle with the fashion establishment of the day and to give back to women the easy-fitting lines that had made her famous. Her timing was

Balenciaga moved away from the very fitted silhouette and developed his semi-fitted line – the first really original fashion concept after the Second World War.

excellent. There was great nostalgia for the 20s and many of France's designers, particularly Balenciaga and Givenchy, were already promoting easier, less fitted clothes.

Press reviews of Chanel's first post-war collection were – to say the least – mixed. Her designs looked as if she had taken up where she had left off; suits had shoulder-pads and her skirts were slightly flared. By 50s' standards, when shoulders were always unpadded and skirts were either very narrow or very full, Chanel's designs looked old-ladyish. After a shaky start, she got back into her stride as a designer. Fashion moved decidedly her way, and her casual, cardigan-style evening suits made in creamy-coloured brocade and edged in navy and gold, or dark red and gold braid, looked effortlessly chic and became a glamour favourite of the late 50s. Chanel was at the beginning of her second period as a major influence on fashion.

The Chanel revival extended the already impressive range of Paris couture. Italy – like England – had its own well respected couturiers, in particular Simenetta, her husband Fabiani and Irene Galatzine. They were admired for their elegant, individual styles and had an international following, but they were not in the same league as the famous Paris designers, and Italy had yet to establish itself as a world leader of high fashion for women.

Away from the rarefied atmosphere of couture, changes were beginning to take place in less formalised fashions and Italy was becoming known for a more glamorous approach to casual-wear and shoe design.

A sexier image for everyday casual clothes was shown off by some of the new Italian film stars. Sophia Loren and Gina Lollobrigida were noted for their well-rounded figures, slightly tousled hairstyles and sensual Latin looks. With brightly-printed silk blouses, off-the-shoulder knitwear and curvy, low-necked tops tucked into wide-belted, hip-clinging skirts or tight-fitting, narrow-legged trousers, slit at the ankles, they presented a franker, easy-to-wear kind of glamour which appealed to the freer attitudes that many of the younger generation were beginning to adopt.

Shoes in the early 50s featured more quiet, conventional styles compared to earlier and later periods. Classic court shoes with moderately shaped toes and unexaggerated high heels were the predominant designs and complemented the strongly stated silhouettes of the time. Strappy, high-heeled sandals and mules were popular alternatives to wear with dressy day outfits and evening wear, and flat ballet-type pumps – worn with tapered trousers or very full skirts – were a teenage favourite.

Italy steadily built up its reputation for shoe design and refined workmanship and in the middle of the decade launched a much more exaggerated basic shape. Toes were elongated into 'winkle-picker' points and very high heels were tapered into knife-sharp 'stilettos'. Despite the obvious disadvantages of a toe-crippling fit with hazardously thin heels, and much condemnation from chiropodists, it proved one of the most successful shoe fashions of the century. It established Italy for directional shoe design to such an extent that elegant, fashion-conscious footwear was always assumed to have 'made in Italy' labels and pointed-toe, stiletto-heel court and T-strap shoes, often in patent leather, became an important part of later 50s glamour dressing.

Age divisions in following fashion had only changed and developed slightly from the attitudes of the 30s and seem quaint by today's standards. The high-fashion ideal was still not young – the dressed-up style of the sophisticated 30s had been replaced by the cooler elegance of the 50s – but the age group portrayed by the designers and presented by the famous model girls remained the same – 30-ish, even though many of the models were in fact only in their early 20s.

The fashion image of the older woman as presented by designers was not as grand and dowager-like as it had been (perhaps the War and the austerity years were thought to have taken a toll on women's energy reserves) and the post-war look was often distinctly comfy and 'grannyish'.

English *Vogue* ran a regular feature on clothes for older women called 'Mrs Exeter, Our Heroine of Fifty-odd'. Compared to many 50-year-olds of the 90s, her appearance resembled that of a 70-year-old. Advice on suitable clothes for the autumn, including an interview with the imaginary Mrs Exeter started: '"I am expecting to spend most of this winter in my own home," said Mrs Exeter, laying skeins of coloured wool neatly along the arm of her chair.' Looking at the clothes recommended for the Mrs Exeters of the 50s – dark button-through dresses, solid-looking tweed suits

Left: Givenchy's simple, elegant 1956 balldress offered a younger look.

with pleated skirts and beret-style hats trimmed with feathers and veiling – it is evident that they were guaranteed to put years on even the most attractive middle-aged woman.

There were, of course, well-dressed, glamorous-looking women in the 50-plus age group; some of them were, as always, admired and valued couture customers, but even designer fashions of the period didn't help them to look young for their years, as they were to do in later decades.

The younger end of fashion – teenage dressing – was beginning to show the greatest potential for change. Young fashion as a separate section, which had started in America, was well-established in many countries by the mid-50s. The

classic, early teenage image of girls with swinging ponytails, tightly-fitted bodices, waists clinched-in with wide elastic belts and very full skirts, swirling out to show layers of petticoats in a 50s jive, had already emerged and was the new post-war equivalent to the flappers with their long beads and fringed chemise dresses shaking out in the 20s charleston.

Although teenage fashions were more lighthearted and colourful, with their bright checks and prints, they were still not truly uninhibited. Buttoned-up, full-skirted dresses with well-below-the-knee hemlines and crisply-laundered white collars, worn with short white gloves, neat shoes and crescent-shaped hats for special occasions, retained the

Left: Couture chic of the mid-50s showed the less tightly-fitted, longer-torsoed silhouette.

'goody-goody' style of an older person's idea of how cute teenagers should dress, rather than expressing the way young people really wanted to look.

Some teenage boys began to copy their older brothers and wore greased-back hair, leather jackets and jeans, and showed a more rebellious spirit than the girls. They were an early pointer to the fashion revolution that was to permanently change the whole concept of teenage dressing.

The post-war revival in fashion and glamour became less remote and more democratic with the growing affluence of the 50s. Mass-produced clothes improved and wholesale manufacturers, with their skilled pattern-cutters, adapted

Right: Dior, nearly a decade after his sensational 'New Look', was following the trend for easier-fitting clothes.

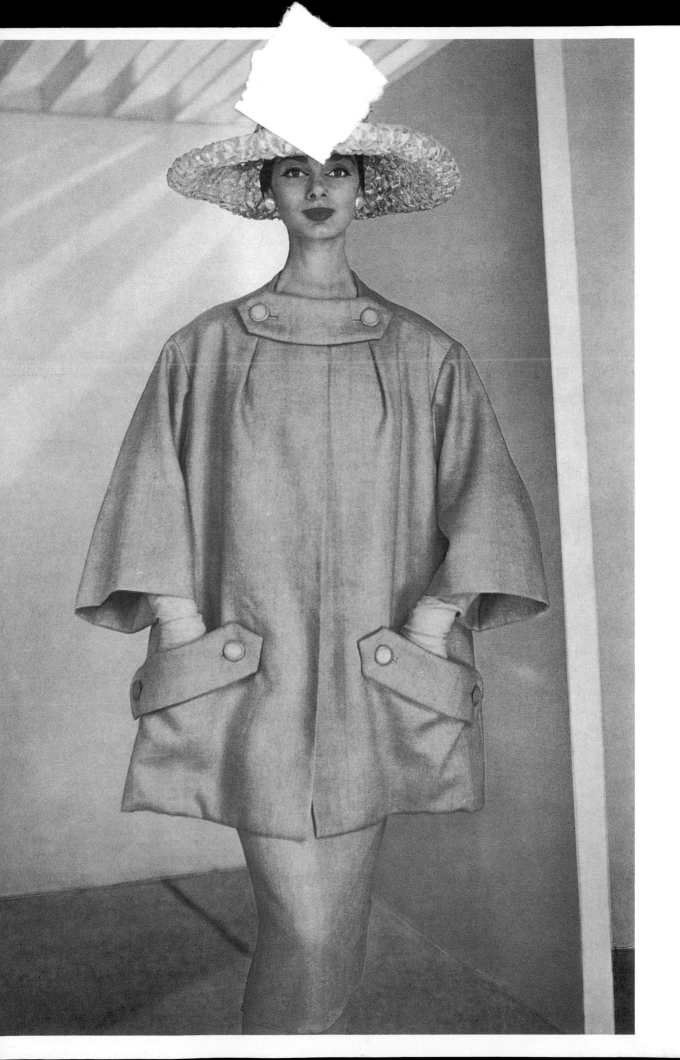

with only slight modifications the high-fashion lines of the leading designers every season. Media coverage made women very conscious of changing fashions and details, such as the exact position of waistlines and the correct lengths for skirts (always quoted as so many inches from the ground). Never before had the latest trends been as readily available in all price ranges and followed by as many women.

Filmstar-style glamour was also not as exclusive as it had been in previous decades. Make-up skills, well-cut hair-styles and figure shaping were all much more within the grasp of post-war women with their increased spending power.

Acquiring the fashionable figure was a great preoccu-

pation and was usually achieved in the traditional way by undergarments specially designed to contort and contain. Women who were confident with their shape had a better-than-ever opportunity to show them off and inspired songwriters of the time to pen such classics as 'Itsy Bitsy, Teeny Weeny, Yellow Polka Dot Bikini'.

Although some men worked out regularly in gyms and exercise programmes were followed by both sexes, the idea of extensive body culture and carefully considered diets to

Above: Marilyn Monroe, with her appealing combination of sexiness and innocence, became the most famous female glamour icon of the 20th century.

enhance looks, figure, health and general well-being, was still in its infancy. After the deprivations of war and recession, many countries were thoroughly enjoying a decade of indulgent eating, and caring parents often thought a diet rich in butter, cream and red meat would help to build a strong, healthy generation.

Sunbathing was also generally considered healthy; deeply-tanned skins were more fashionable than ever and less of a status symbol as many more people could afford to take holidays in sunny climates.

Well-publicised fashion trends for men as a clear parallel to women's, which became established from the 60s onwards, had started in the first half of the 50s, and young men from all sections in society were already becoming less reticent in showing a more obvious interest in following fashion.

The 50s were in many ways the beginning of the 'modern age', the following decades produced great changes, shocks and upheavals but it was a continuing process and was less obviously divided by world events than the earlier part of the century.

Rising living standards in many parts of the world and popular mass culture really got underway during the 50s; social attitudes were changing and fashion and glamour, which had been out of reach for so many, became more commercially available and so lost some of their mystique and fantasy appeal. Glamour's 'golden age', which had lasted for nearly 30 years, was becoming out-dated by the times, and was about to be revised by new concepts to greet the arrival of the 'pop age'.

Section Two
Glamour in the Pop Age

Major social changes, radically different ideals and values – germinating for several years in the free world – burst forth in the late 50s.

Glamour Revised

The late 50s and early 60s

The new generation in their teens and early 20s were less affected by preconceptions about society and the status quo between nations. They were too young to remember life before the Second World War, only had childhood memories of the War and austerity years, and had grown up accepting the Cold War, the welfare state, full employment and growing affluence as facts of life. They were one of the most fortunate generations of the century with greater opportunities than ever before to pursue personal ambitions and fulfil their individual potentials.

There were many more students from modest backgrounds at universities and colleges; creativity was coming from all sections of society and a new vitality was affecting writing, design and music. Pop music was the mass communicator which cut across society and nationalities with even greater force than jazz had in the 20s.

Couture high fashion and glitzy film-star glamour, which had been supreme for so long, seemed to have run out of fresh-looking innovation. It had become part of the establishment and – to many of the young – a middle-aged concept for well-preserved mothers.

The new trendsetters had no admiration for the glossy and the groomed, the immaculately turned-out or the well-mannered style of dressing. They thought ball dresses and tuxedos were for 'squares' and glamour in fashion had to be revised to 'get with it'.

Opposite: Brigitte Bardot's looks and 'sex kitten' image had a great influence on young fashions in clothes, hairstyles and make-up.

The range of male sex symbols and commercialised, sexy glamour looks for men, so unremarkable today, started in the late 50s and the early 60s, and was the biggest change in the concept of men's appearance for over a hundred years. Pop singers in their early 20s, some of whom were to become megastars within a few years, were the new style leaders; like female film stars, they had the power to influence fashion trends – any style they adopted immediately became a part of their individual image.

Elvis Presley, a good-looking, fresh-faced 22-year-old, in the 1957 film *Loving You*, played a character not unlike himself, a country-boy singer who becomes a famous rock 'n' roll star. His style presentation: jet-black hair greased into a quiff with medium length sideboards, classic denim shirts and T-shirts, tight-fitting jeans belted in with a fancy Western belt, worn over cowboy boots, was a much more overtly sexy look for the time. It was emphasised by Elvis's famous pelvic thrust movements as he sang his latest hits to ecstatic teenage audiences. The older generation disapproved, the media called him 'Elvis the Pelvis' and the early Elvis look made a lasting impression. It became one of the classic 20th-century looks, enduringly popular with generations of stars and the general public alike and it can still be seen in countless high streets today.

As Elvis demonstrated, hair was an important part of male glamour and other stars of the late 50s – Bill Haley of Bill Haley and his Comets, one of the original rockers (famed for the hits 'Rock Around the Clock' and 'Shake Rattle and Roll'), the Everly Brothers and Britain's Cliff Richard, all wore their hair styled rather than cut-and-shaped. It was left long on top, usually greased, parted or taken back and combed into high side-sweeps and carefully-arranged pompadour waves, designed to flop forward as they sang. Pocket combs were carried at all times and frequent combing to keep the style arrangement in place was a common characteristic of the time.

The new pop-star idols, particularly Elvis Presley, introduced a much more overtly sexy image for young men.

Pictures of the Beatles at the beginning of the 60s, playing as a Hamburg-based group, moody-looking in their leather phase also showed them with high-swept, rocker hairstyles. Two years later, they had a very different cut, shaped to fall back in place after much 'shaking out' during their stage performances. It was part of a new image – sharp, collarless, wool jackets and neatly-pressed matching tapered trousers worn with elastic-gussetted Chelsea boots which replaced the leather-boy look. The boys were already famous enough at this time for their hairstyle to be called 'The Beatle Cut' (with 'Beatle fringes' particularly popular), their jackets 'Beatle Jackets' and their boots renamed 'Beatle

Right: Balenciaga's and Givenchy's 1957 leggy, unfitted line was a complete reversal of the hour-glass shape of a few years before.

Left: Spring 1958 – the trapeze line. Yves St Laurent's younger-looking first solo collection for Dior.

Opposite (top left and main pic):
Yves St Laurent's early designs for
his own couture house included the
easy-fitting tunic line.

Opposite (middle pic): Britain's
Henrietta Tiarks (now Lady
Tavistock), one of the most
beautiful debutantes of the late 50s,
displayed a very style-conscious
image with her fashionably-full
hair and dramatic evening dress.

Opposite (bottom left): Givenchy's
simple suits and sheath dresses were
glamorised with jewellery and
sophisticated hairstyles.

This page: Pierre Cardin's bloused-
back oval-shapes, in fruit-drop
colours, were described by the press
as 'futuristic and space-age'.

Boots' – styles which became some of the most copied of the decade, destined to feature in many family albums (often to the embarrassment of fathers when their youthful image was discovered by curious offspring in later years).

Strutting, preening pop-star heroes introduced a new body-consciousness, different from the broad-shouldered, wide-chested, 'beefcake' ideal of the 40s and early 50s, and the serious body development of present day work-out programmes.

Thirty years ago, the body ideal was very young, almost adolescent. Even the beach-boy physiques of young actors, like teenage heart-throb Tab Hunter, were slim rather than hunky (Tab Hunter's hairstyle, cut into a short, even 'college boy', was also widely copied). Fashionable clothes emphasised the boyish figure – jackets were cut narrow and were high fastening, shirts were less full with small, button-down collars and very slim trousers broke over ankle-covering boots to give a long, leggy line. The shape of men's legs was shown off more revealingly than at any time since the age of the dandy at the beginning of the 19th century.

Young, style-conscious men in the 60s squeezed themselves into pants that by both earlier and later standards would have been considered far too small; they were supposed to look as tight as possible and clearly show the thighs, buttocks and legs. The obsession with fit led some as far as shrinking jeans to the figure in the bath, and lying on the floor to pull the zip closed. Burst seams were not unusual and P. J. Proby, a successful pop star of the time, split open his back trouser-seam during an energetic stage routine and in so doing made the front page of many newspapers. Tight pants looked good on the young and slim but were devastatingly awful on many middle-aged 'trendies'.

Sean Connery was only in his early 30s when he became famous for his James Bond rôle. Although he played a character who was tough, ruthless and promiscuous, he was perfectly acceptable to the changed social attitudes. His dark good looks, success with beautiful women and his sexy, groomed appearance – silk suits, pale blue voile shirts, narrow navy silk ties and soft, black leather slip-on shoes – all epitomised the smooth, sophisticated 60s man of the world.

In contrast to the fastidious James Bond image, vaguely anti-establishment cult dressing was a growing influence. 'Beatniks', or members of the 'beat generation', originated in America. They were poets, writers, artists and musicians who disassociated themselves from the aims of contemporary society, had a disrespect for the conventional way of life, and tended to dwell on a kind of grainy realism which was reflected in their careless appearance: pallid faces, unstyled hair and dark clothes (usually black and grey), baggy sweaters, aged leather jackets and waistcoats and well-worn, scuffed boots under or pulled over narrow cord or denim jeans.

Commercialised versions of beatnik-inspired styles were a popular feature of young fashion in the late 50s and early 60s, and were early examples of how cult and street dressing would be adapted and refined for the mainstream fashion market.

Beat boys wore longer hair with thicker sideboards and black polo-neck sweaters, boxy leather jackets and dark grey or grey-and-black-striped, narrow-legged jeans over unpolished Chelsea or calf-length boots. Their female counterparts, with heavily made-up eyes and pale lips, wore their hair in arranged disarray, softly piled on top of a centre-parted or irregular-shaped fringe and loosely pinned into a French pleat or – in classic 60s style – hair was allowed to fall loose and straight onto the shoulders from a smooth, centre parting.

Leather jackets or waistcoats and dark sweaters were also popular with girls. Black polo-necks were often worn under grey, easy-fitting pinafore dresses with knee-length hemlines, black stockings and high, black leather boots. Beat

A very characteristic Mary Quant design – grey-and-black striped pinafore dress over the indispensable black polo-neck.

girls looked rather like naughty teenage schoolgirls who had used too much eye make-up and borrowed their brothers' sweaters and leather jackets.

There were much more experimental, less inhibited attitudes towards dress. Male pop stars were role models for young men, and young women looked with great interest at the newly emerging creative talents in fashion that were to revise and redefine the whole concept of glamour.

Britain in the late 50s was known for its good quality, timeless classics – knitwear, raincoats, bespoke tailoring and couturiers who catered for the traditional social life of the establishment. Thus, London's radical, youth-orientated fashions were an exciting new development.

Chelsea's Kings Road was an ordinary south London high street of family shops when Mary Quant and her husband – Alexander – opened their first boutique, *Bazaar*, there in the mid-50s, selling well-chosen, modern-looking designs from progressive wholesale manufacturers.

Mary soon felt that she couldn't find the really advanced styling she believed in for her adventurous young clientele and started to produce her own designs. Her instincts were right. The clothes were instantly successful and became the hallmark of the avant-garde Chelsea set – a second *Bazaar* shop soon opened in Knightsbridge. They were the new fashion meccas for the ultra style conscious; their windows always drew interest and admiration and they rapidly became internationally known.

Mary and Alexander were a glamorous, confident couple in their mid-20s. Mary, like Chanel, was a wonderful advertisement for her own designs; her short, dark bob with its schoolgirl fringe and her easy-fitting, young-looking blazer jackets, brief, swinging skirts and pinafore dresses suited her perfectly. Tall, good-looking Alexander was elegantly modern in his narrow, high-buttoning jackets and very slim, tapered trousers.

Quant designs were slightly influenced by beat dressing

A glamorous and confident Mary Quant and her husband, Alexander, with a selection of Mary's 'Ginger Group' range.

but interpreted in a more considered, sharper, varied style. Her concept was uncompromisingly young – ten years younger than the long-established, high-fashion ideal. She designed for a girlish, less developed figure; her dresses had simple, boat-shaped necklines or rather childlike, round or pointed collars and narrow shoulders and sleeves. Summer and evening dresses were frequently sleeveless and body-shaping was very understated, shadowing the breasts and waist to give a long-torsoed, slightly 20s silhouette with hip-level belts and seaming. The long-waisted look made her flared and pleated skirts, with their just-above-the-knee lengths, look even shorter; they were in fact the shortest on record, beating the highest hemlines of the 1920s by a couple of inches, and were worn with simple, strap-over shoes or long boots.

Fashion shows in the 50s were usually accompanied by rather flowery commentaries and at couture shows each outfit was given a number and a high society name such as 'The Ritz', 'The Waldorf', 'Ascot' or 'Langchamps'. At the beginning of Mary Quant's shows, a cool-looking Alexander announced that there would be no commentary or descriptions 'because Mary's designs speak for themselves' – and they did. Models sauntered up and down the catwalk, looking as if they really believed in and enjoyed wearing the clothes they were presenting; the styles epitomised the new mood in fashion and the audiences watched every outfit with rapt attention.

Mary Quant did many aspiring designers a great favour. Her publicity and success made traditionally cautious manufacturers alter their attitudes and want their own creative designers whose style would appeal to the newly important, big-spending 16–25-year-olds.

Madge Garland, the first Professor of Fashion at London's Royal College of Art, who had set up the fashion school so professionally in the late 40s, retired in 1956 and was succeeded by a very youthful-looking Janey Ironside.

The pretty 'dolly-girl' dress was a very popular young fashion of the early 60s.

Janey, with her sensitive, pale looks, casual but fashionably full, dark hair, simple, knee-length chemise dresses and pointed stilettos, was frequently mistaken for one of her own students.

Her vocation for the job probably surprised even Janey herself. She had a rare ability to be able to encourage and foster her students' individual style and talent without imposing on them her own taste and design preferences. She cared about her students, and some of them, including Sally Tuffin and Marion Foale, Roger Nelson, Bill Gibb, Christopher McDonnell, Ossie Clark and Anthony Price, became well-known designers within a year or two of leaving the College, running their own businesses whilst still in their early or mid-20s.

David Sassoon, who had always liked a more traditional type of glamour than many of his fellow students, became the designer for Belinda Bellville, specialising in debutantes' clothes and wedding dresses. His less strictly traditional, younger, more original designs, were soon noticed; Bellville expanded to become a much more extensive couture house, dressing many members of the Royal Family (including, in more recent years, the Princess of Wales) and acquiring an impressive international clientele. Today, Bellville/Sassoon, with its couture and ready-to-wear styles, is run by David Sassoon, one of the Royal College's most enduring design talents.

Two other British designers destined to become fashion doyennes of the 70s, 80s and 90s – Zandra Rhodes and Jean Muir – also embarked on their careers in the 60s.

Zandra, originally a textile student at the Royal College of Art, established the idea that fabric interest – as opposed to intricate design – could be stunningly effective. Her dramatic, flowing dresses, often with their sleeves cut in one to form a sweeping batwing-shape, were primarily designed to show off her unique prints, with their daring use of colour and seemingly inexhaustible range of inventive design

themes. Zandra's fashion shows always resembled exciting, colourful stage productions; her highly individual style made her world famous and the designs became collectors' pieces. Her own appearance proclaimed her fashion philosophy – hair brightly coloured with reds, greens and blues (sometimes all at once), and face unabashedly made-up to look theatrical with spikey eye decoration, heavy blusher and specks of glitter. Wearing brilliant prints, she caused much head-turning wherever she went and received considerable publicity; always easy to pick out at a party, she was ahead of her time, a glamorous punk rocker long before punk became a fashion influence.

Jean Muir's style was very different. She designed for Jaeger and a young fashion firm of the early 60s, Jane and Jane, before opening her own business, actively encouraged and assisted by her husband. She believed in understatement and the evolution of cut. Her clothes were quiet looking, often in dark colours, particularly navy and black, and made in supple fabrics like crêpe and jersey. Women loved wearing Jean Muir clothes which reflected a Parisian understanding of cut and drape (in the tradition of Chanel and Vionnet) that was unusual for a British designer. They flattered the figure without emphasising it; the natural lines of the shoulders and arms looked appealingly feminine and slender but unrestricted, and fabric flowed rather than clung, outlining the breasts, waist and hips. Muir designs managed to be womanly and slim – they moved well and had an underplayed glamour, flattering to women of all ages. Jean Muir devotees have remained enthusiastic throughout the decades.

The 60s was London's decade. It was just the right time and place for the new British style to succeed and become an international influence. The young from all classes, with full employment and minimal overheads, had more disposable income than ever before and spent a high proportion of it on their appearance. Designers, hairdressers, photogra-

phers and retailers were able to start their own businesses with very modest capital in a way that would not be possible today, and in doing so were free to express their individual style and chart their own course.

The style setters – all under 30 years old – interacted well together. Hairdressers created styles that complemented the designers' ideas – Vidal Sassoon's sculptured

bobs were exactly right for Mary Quant's clothes. Jean Shrimpton ('The Shrimp') was only 17 when she started modelling; at 19 she was famous, jetting around the world to be photographed in exciting locations, wearing the kind of modern clothes she would probably have chosen for herself.

David Bailey's *Vogue* pictures were causing a stir by the

Left: Although far less popular than in earlier decades, the big glamour hat was still stunningly effective for special-occasion dressing.

Above: Jean Shrimpton, 'The Shrimp', was one of the best-known models of the 60s and was world-famous before she reached her 20th birthday.

time he was 23. He photographed fashion in a way that had not been known before, replacing the aloofness of early models with the coltish, leggy looks of girls like Jean Shrimpton, who related to the new mood in fashion. They were shown as free spirits – sitting on the floor, showing lots of leg, running through fields with their hair ruffled by the wind, wearing skimpy, girlish dresses in daisy prints with crocheted collars, or marching down sombre streets in stormtroopers' leather trenchcoats and jackboots. Images ranged from the sweet and innocent to the baby-doll tease and the frankly erotic.

The obvious glamour appeal of leather-wear and boots, admired and perfectly acceptable as part of military uniforms, and motorbike-gear, were still considered daring when adopted for everyday wear; fetishist innuendos were sniggered over and simple leather coats, jackets and boots were often called 'kinky leather gear'. 'Kinky boots' were immortalised in song and Nancy Sinatra had a worldwide hit with the thumping 'These Boots Are Made For Walking', in 1966.

The British influence did much to revise the image of glamour in fashion. It changed more in three or four years than was usual in a decade, became youth-dominated, experimental, irreverent, more 'trendy boutique' than 'haute couture' and sexier – 'cool chick' or 'dolly bird' rather than 'sophisticated lady'.

International interest fuelled by the success of British pop groups, particularly the Beatles, focused on London and its new style as never before; the press and the fashion buyers arrived in force, while newspapers and magazines ran many features on the explosion of British talent. The American media, always quick to capture the public's imagination, labelled it 'Swinging London', and named an era for the history books.

America was still Europe's most important export market for fashion; US buyers had considerable purchasing power and regular trips to London went on many more schedules and were no longer confined to buying only classic clothes.

It was a heady time for Britain's young designers with their merchandise being ordered for coast to coast US distribution. Small businesses were sometimes overwhelmed by the quantities demanded and instant expansion was thrust upon them. Designers were taken on nationwide promotional trips across the States and contracted to design special ranges for American stores and manufacturers. At home, even more orders flooded in. Boutiques clamouring to sell young designs mushroomed along Carnaby Street in the West End (first known for selling trendy menswear) and Chelsea's Kings Road. They also opened in many towns and cities throughout Britain.

Across the Channel, Paris acknowledged the change in British fashion and many of the young admired the anti-establishment 'cool' of the Chelsea look.

France in the early 60s, troubled by political and social unrest as she decolonised her North African territories, was going through a crisis of confidence, and General de Gaulle made his famous rallying 'aidez-moi' speech on television.

Paris couture was also going through a kind of crisis of confidence. The establishment houses, Dior, Balenciaga, Balmain and Nina Ricci, continued to produce flattering, tasteful, beautifully-made clothes for a receptive international market of affluent women who preferred to stay with the traditional chic of French couture. The designers, however, no longer had the authority to dictate fashion changes as they had a few years earlier, when eager buyers and press waited to be given the 'correct' skirt length and the exact details of new silhouettes.

The fashionable lines of the early 60s – simple shift dresses and semi-fitted tailoring – were easily-produced basic shapes for wholesale manufacturers, and the French ready-to-wear, led by young designers like Emmanuelle

Khanh, were becoming a growing fashion influence. Pared-down silhouettes were harder for couturiers to make appear richly glamorous and it was left to the youngest and oldest designers of Paris to update and secure French supremacy in high fashion.

Yves St Laurent was a 22-year-old understudy when Christian Dior died in 1957 and the awesome mantle of producing the Dior collections fell on his shoulders. At first, he gave a younger slant to the established Dior image but his 1959/60 'beat' collections were much more controversial.

His beehive-shaped hats, high, topknot-dressed hair, multi-stranded 'choker' necklaces, extensive use of black for leather blouson jackets, wool jackets cropped at the waist and bubble-shaped skirts caught into a hobble-band visibly baring the knees, caused an outcry. They were not considered in the tradition of couture or the sort of clothes Dior's valued clientele were used to. Critical views declared them suitable for daughters to buy from a Left Bank boutique, but not for presenting to their chic mothers in Dior's salon. *Vogue* came to St Laurent's defence and, in a lead article, pointed out: 'When a new line is greeted with cries of indignation, it's a healthy sign. It means change and new ideas, it means that the fashion world is alive and kicking, ready to shock us into new awareness.'

Yves St Laurent had a difficult couple of years ahead. Conflicts of style at Dior were followed by his nervous exhaustion, which led to him being invalided out of military service. By 1962 his career was back on course; he had his own fashion house where he was free to express his more modern style. This was the beginning of his long reign as one of the most respected and influential designers of the later 20th century.

Pierre Cardin was another young designer who became known for his advanced styling, described by the press as 'futuristic' and 'space-age'. His fruitdrop colours – orange, lemon, strawberry and lime – added impact to his very new-looking designs, which featured shapes that were not directly related to the curves of the female figure. Basic knee-length chemises and easy-fitting coats and jackets curved or bloused out at the back and then tapered in to form an oval shape, while high-waisted dresses and skirts ballooned into soft bubbles gathered under at the hemline.

Other designers and fashion students admired and were influenced by Cardin's bold new shapes. Although his style never became as abstract or extreme as his early collections might have suggested, his designs have always been forward-looking with their skilful, inventive cut and the drama of futuristic styling. Influenced by this, the glamour of fictitious space-age heroes became an important fashion trend of the late 60s.

For a woman over 70, whose style was closely associated with a bygone age, to be able to re-establish her position as one of the most important couturiers by recycling her original concept, would be a considerable achievement at any time. For Coco Chanel to do this in the youth-obsessed 1960s was truly remarkable.

Chanel had introduced women to the effortless ease of the cardigan jacket, the soft blouse and the gently-flared skirt in the 20s. She successfully reintroduced them to it 30 years later and, by the early 60s, the 'Chanel Look', epitomised by her suits, had emerged as one of the most popular commercial fashions of the decade.

Chanel suits of the 60s remain clearly recognisable as earlier versions of a perennial favourite. Fabric interest with clever contrasting trimmings featured then as they do today. Easy-fitting jackets in soft-handling woollens and tweeds, edged with fancy braiding or trimmed with silk revers, often in contrasting colours – navy on pink, red, green or cream (and cream on navy) – fastened with gilt or fabric-covered buttons, were worn with silky blouses in toning colours. Chanel blouses had simple neckbands or scarf collars tied over and held with a jewelled pin, or arranged in a floppy bow. Slightly flared skirts were cut in panels, with slit pockets in the front panels or the side seams.

To complete the Chanel look, casual, fringed hairstyles were tied at the nape of the neck with a silk bow, or small pillbox hats, covered in the same fabric as the suit, were worn on the back of the head. Gilt chains were worn hanging round the neck, hooked through the belt loops of skirts and used for the handles of quilted leather handbags. The outfits were finished off with high-heeled slingback sandals which had black leather or silk toecaps and beige suede uppers.

Chanel's style suited all ages, was kind to the figure and, above all, fulfilled a need. In a time of experimental and rather severe lines, her clothes were softer and more flattering while remaining suitable for a faster moving way of life, and could be worn for many occasions during the day and on into the evening.

Jackie Kennedy, a fashion leader of the early 60s, illustrated the appeal of the Chanel image, and looked pretty and feminine in her Chanel-style suit, unaware that her choice of clothes would be tragically recorded for the history books with the assassination of her husband, President John F. Kennedy, on their tour of Texas in November 1963.

Another Frenchwoman, young enough to be Chanel's granddaughter, was also having a great influence on fashion and the way women looked. Brigitte Bardot became well-known for her so-called 'sex kitten' roles. In films like *And God Created Woman* she played a girl-woman, innocently unsophisticated and yet knowing, coy one moment and sensual and sexually-aware the next.

In the early years of this more liberated era, Bardot, like David Bailey's photographic models, presented a powerful new fantasy image; men looked for 'Bardot girls' and young women all over the world aspired to her style.

Like Marilyn Monroe, she rejected the contrived artifice of the old style, expensively dressed-up movie star in favour of showing off her youthful looks and superbly-proportioned figure in casual, clingy young fashions. Her hair, which got progressively blonder over the months, was worn in a soft, loosely-arranged beehive, centre parted, drawn across the forehead and allowed to partly cascade down onto the shoulders. In stark contrast to all the blondeness, Bardot's make-up concentrated fashionably on the eyes, which were outlined darkly and heavily eyelashed.

Scoop-necked T-shirts and dresses emphasised the breasts and were belted into a small waist. Tight trousers and narrow slit skirts showed slim but well-shaped hips. Her short, bouffant-skirted, pink-and-white-checked gingham dress – girlishly trimmed with white *broderie-anglaise* – worn with a matching gingham or pink chiffon headscarf, tied over her beehive hair to knot under the chin, angled sunglasses and white pointed-toe stilettos, was one of the most popular fashion images of the late 50s.

Lookalike Bardots in gingham, riding pillion behind Italian-jacketed boyfriends on their Vespas, were a familiar sight on the streets of London, Paris and Rome.

Brigitte Bardot was closely associated with the glamorous but more laid-back lifestyle of the rich and famous in the South of France. St Tropez was at its peak as the most fashionable Mediterranean resort and its reputation was further enhanced when Bardot made her principal home there.

Resort-wear was a growing influence on casual clothes and St Tropez's boutiques launched many fashion trends. Attractive, tanned young people paraded past the harbourside cafés, showing off the latest styles, watched by equally goodlooking contemporaries wearing the same 'in' looks. Bare-midriff tops and low-cut, Western-style, unisex hipster trousers, worn with wide belts high on the hips and finishing just above the ankle, were succeeded by the same basic cut but one which flared into bell-bottoms below the knee.

Despite the crowds, the lack of space and the heat, boy and girl biker 'posers' roared around the narrow streets, or

In the 60s, the evening-wear image
for hair and make-up was younger
and less strictly formal.

parked in groups on the harbourside and sat astride their motorbikes, showing off their clothes. They were much more chic than the average urban 'ton-up' kid and wore expensive, designer-style, soft, black leather jackets teamed with immaculate white T-shirts (flattering to the tan) and pressed, faded blue jeans rolled up to show imported, tooled-leather, American cowboy boots.

In contrast to the predominance of trousers and jeans, girls returning from the beach wore thigh-length, pretty, flowery, printed cotton tunics or smocks (often in voile), tied on the shoulders, which veiled bikinis in a matching print. The beach-tops looked cool and feminine, very suitable for wearing around the resort – they were the early forerunners of the mid-60s mini-dresses.

On the nearby Tahiti beach, dauntingly-beautiful, golden-brown females displayed the latest in minimal bikinis while the *really* daring were peeling off to sunbathe topless.

The always slender Audrey Hepburn, admired since the early 50s for her great sense of style, portrayed new glamour ideals in the charming 1961 film *Breakfast at Tiffanys*. She played a young woman with a split personality – half Manhattan sophisticate, half country-girl waif. Her clothes reflected both characters and, at the same time, two contrasting fashion looks. Givenchy's slightly high-waisted or low-flounced shift dresses in black, accessorised with expensive jewelled earrings, dark glasses, deep-crowned, important-looking hats, long gloves and court shoes were all perfect for high-profile appearances. Evening dresses were even more stunning – ankle-length, black sheath dresses or short-skirted bubble dresses in shocking pink were worn with glittering jewels and high top-knot hairstyles. For further effect, a long cigarette-holder was carried, waved about and generally posed with.

For a much quieter, underplayed lifestyle, a less made-up, younger-looking, pony-tailed Hepburn was just as appealing in a loose, cowl-necked mohair sweater, dark tapered trousers and flat ballet pumps, or in a short, tightly-belted beige trench coat and silk headscarf worn 60s style – wrapped round the head and knotted at the back – together with the indispensable dark glasses.

Age grouping in fashion changed radically in the 60s. Teenage, young and advanced high fashion all merged into the general style image of the period which was resolutely youthful – the ideal age for wearing the strongly-stated looks was about 19. Older women felt left out and complained that there was nothing for them and that they were excluded from the whole contemporary fashion picture. In fact, many manufacturers still specialised in clothes for the older woman, but they tended to stay with variations on styles that had been established in the 50s.

Chanel presented the solution. Her suits and coats were both flatteringly youthful and appropriate and were widely copied in all price ranges. A Chanel suit with a noticeably shorter but not-too-short hemline, going hatless and concentrating on a more modern, slightly lifted hairstyle all worked wonders for mature looks and successfully updated the appearance of many fashion-conscious older women.

Marlene Dietrich, in her late 50s and early 60s, was a shining example of the perpetuation of a glamour image. On and off the screen she still looked the archetypal movie star in immaculate couture suits, furs, glittering evening dresses and jewels. In a more casual, youth-orientated age, her aura of traditional glamour held a nostalgic appeal for all generations, which guaranteed her admiring capacity audiences on her cabaret tours of Europe and the States.

In a subtle way her continuing success had been helped by cleverly updating her established style. She revised her make-up emphasis, rarely wore hats and, although she kept the basic concept of a floppy, medium-length bob, it was a fuller, slightly bouffant 60s version. Her fabulous legs, still in stunning shape, were more on view than ever in knee-skimming hemlines and her figure-moulding, embroidered evening dresses, flatteringly veiling the arms and shoulders in chiffon, were decorated at the neck and wrists with eye-catching jewels.

Dietrich showed how glamour looks could be extended further than most women had dared to hope. However, her appearance acknowledged ways to soften and minimise signs of ageing, in contrast to some present day attitudes which decisively reject any acceptance of advancing age and strive to physically combat its effects.

The new young film stars of the early 60s – Hollywood's Ursula Andress, Raquel Welch, Natalie Wood and Warren Beatty, together with Britain's classless Julie Christie and the working-class hero, Terence Stamp – were all admired role models for looks, figure and mannerisms, but unlike earlier stars they were not promoted as important fashion leaders.

Style inspiration was more diverse. Couture, boutique and ready-to-wear designers, pop stars, movie stars, hair-dressers, photographers, model girls and cult dressing all had an input and helped to give a less dictatorial and more democratic range of younger fashion looks.

For all the casualness of the young, make-up was as important as ever and continued to concentrate on the eyes, which were always strongly outlined and often shaded with layers of false lashes. 'Putting the eyes on' and maintaining them throughout the day was a priority for 60s girls; the reassurance of dramatically made-up eyes was as important to them as the heavily lipsticked mouth had been to their mothers. Hairstyling for men and women was a very important part of their individual image and hairdressing boomed as never before.

Apart from traditional 'country set' tweed caps and hats and the occasional trendy leather 'Beatle cap', most young men went hatless – in fact, many didn't possess any kind of headgear. Instead, like their girlfriends, they enjoyed a change of image by regularly revising their hairstyles and

went from greased 'rocker pompadours' to neat Californian 'college boy' crops and on to long sideboards and Beatle fringes all within two or three years. Their fathers, who had stayed with the conformist 'short-back-and-sides' cut since boyhood, were astounded by their sons' dandified preoccupation with their hair.

The decline in women's hat-wearing, which had started in the 40s and gathered speed in the 50s, was complete by the early 60s. Although berets and boyish caps were sometimes worn, and fashion magazines continued to feature high-crowned, important-looking hats, they were rarely worn by the young and were reserved more and more for special occasions, such as weddings and christenings.

More complicated hairstyling compensated for the lack of interest in hats. Backcombing and sprayed-on lacquer were characteristic of most women's hairstyles. Towering 'beehives', heightened bobs (cut short in 20s style to curve onto the cheeks, or left long enough to brush smoothly into shoulder-touching 'flick ups'), loose, free-flowing 60s manes falling from moderately full, slightly arranged crowns, all had varying degrees of contrived lift.

Although film stars were still admired for their glamorous, well-proportioned figures, less importance was placed on body development than in earlier or later decades. In fact, there was a complete change of emphasis in less than 10 years. In the first half of the 50s, men had been admired for a broad-shouldered, well-built physique and women for large breasts and small waists. In the 60s, however, figure-shaping for both sexes was more underplayed than at any time since the 1920s, and thighs and legs became the most important features of body show, whether in unisex tight pants or with the sensational shortening of women's hemlines to mini and micro lengths.

Leggy looks made footwear even more important and very much a part of glamour dressing. Young women often bought a new pair of shoes or boots to liven up fashion

Right and opposite: Evening
dresses like these glamorous Nina
Ricci designs related more closely to
the simple day silhouette – richness
and exclusivity was shown in the
use of fabrics, prints and surface
decoration.

Above: Chanel's flattering, soft suits were one of the most popular and commercialised fashions of the period.

interest in their basic outfits, just as earlier generations had done with new hats.

Shoes and boots for both sexes were based on the same elongated shape, tapered into points or finished off with a chiselled-toe effect. Raised stack-heels were a new feature of men's Western- and Chelsea-style boots and the stage-stomping pop star heroes who favoured them appealed to the more extrovert generation who welcomed strongly-stated fashion looks for men.

Women's boots were modelled on classic, pull-on riding boots, adapted to fashionable toe and heel shapes. Flat heels gave a rather Russian look while high, slender heels were more towny and sexy. Black was an established basic, but shiny patents, dark-coloured suedes and 'moc crocs' were also being worn. Bright red boots were the most daring and white boots, despite the effort involved to keep them clean, were surprisingly popular.

In contrast to the equestrian and military influences reflected in boots, women's shoes were ultra-feminine and delicate-looking with narrow toes, medium-height stiletto heels, sling-backs and fine straps decorating low-cut fronts and open sides.

Apart from special occasion jewels, such as glittering, multi-stranded necklaces and matching cluster-shaped ear-rings to wear with dressy evening wear, jewellery, in keeping with the general mood in fashion, was more casual and less pretentious.

Fashionable daytime, rollneck sweaters, collarless jack-ets and boat-shaped necklines on tops and dresses were often left unadorned; when jewellery was added it was usually for its design interest or to give a 'lift' to an outfit, rather than for showing affluence.

Bangles, fake pearls and earth-coloured beads made of wood, or old-fashioned, coloured beads, particularly in blue-green and amber shades (some found neglected in mothers' and grandmothers' jewel boxes) were revived and admired for their period charm. They were worn either as a single long strand (which looked good with unfitted chemises and long-line sweaters) or arranged in several medium-length rows on gently-curved jackets and shift dresses.

By the early 60s, younger looks and easier-fitting lines had affected all areas of fashion. Even establishment dressing, formal outfits and evening wear were less struc-tured and figure constraining.

Evening dresses were not as opulent-looking or as period-costume 'romantic', and related more closely to the simple day silhouettes of the time just as they had done in the 1920s. Sleeveless shift dresses, with boat-shaped neck-lines, or fitted, slightly high-waisted bodices joined to softly gathered bubble or bell-shaped skirts, were the uncluttered, basic shapes, made in a range of hemlines – on-the-knee, to-the-ankle and full-length.

Couture customers, used to built-in bras, boned bodices and huge skirts, noticed the simplicity of the new styles and wondered if the expensive dresses were good value. Richness was shown in fabric and surface decoration. Fitted bodices were often prettily encrusted with glitter and long, elegant shift dresses in jewel-coloured slub silks or dark velvets were heavily-embroidered round the neck. For a softer, very feminine look, layers of smokey-coloured chiffon were used to veil delicately-embroidered, shimmering, ankle-length sheath dresses.

Fur jackets and stoles were less popular and were often replaced by silk evening coats in a matching colour, which were glamorous and practical covers for bare-necked, minimal-sleeved dresses. It was yet another 60s fashion that related to the 20s when flappers had covered their skimpy chemise dresses with cocoon-shaped, silky evening wraps.

Traditional glamour dressing continued into the 60s in a modified form, but it was no longer a directional, inventive force in fashion.

The new style concepts – very fashion-conscious looks

for men; artistry in hair, flatteringly cut and shaped to lift and fall in place and complement heavily made-up eyes; easy, semi-fitted lines for dresses and tailoring; leather in the mainstream of fashion, used for coats, jackets, skirts and trousers; the ever-growing ranks of jeans wearers and trousers as city fashion garments for women, as well as everyday basics (including the first stretch pants); more legginess in shrinking hemlines, showing off black and patterned tights and knee-high boots — were all radical trends 30 years ago. They look less exciting in retrospect because they became establishment fashions of the later part of the century, regularly revamped and relaunched as important looks of a particular season.

Schiaparelli, the big fashion name of the 30s, was unimpressed by the new trends of the late 50s and early 60s and described them as 'apathetic clothes for apathetic times'.

In fact, after 30 years, the glamour ideal had been revised, changed, relaxed, made more casual and become younger and more experimental, reflecting the very different attitudes of the new post-War generation; a prelude leading into the wilder, even more exuberant fashions of the late 60s and early 70s.

Left: Nancy Sinatra displays the fashionable face of the mid-60s — emphasised eyes and pale lips.

Above: The Beatles, role models of a generation. Beatle fringes, suits and boots were all essential features of 'with-it' dressing.

Youth Cults and Fantasy Dressing

The 60s and 70s

SECTION TWO The new youth culture, which dominated fashion and style-conscious living, intensified as the 60s progressed and continued to spread its free-thinking, free-spirited, experimental attitudes. It is difficult to overstate the sheer uninhibited fun and excitement of fashion from the mid-60s to the early 70s – it was unlike anything known before or since. The changes of the previous decade had paved the way and by 1964, the young were receptive to

Opposite: Shimmering 'pop-age' fantasy dress worn by top model of the 60s, Jill Kennington.

ever more radical developments. Fashion — always a reflection of the times — threw away the rulebook, fantasy took over and a succession of 'pop-age' looks followed.

André Courreges's dazzling 'Space-age Look' was one of the first. (It also helped to give the authority of the Paris couture a much needed boost.) Courreges had trained with Balenciaga before opening his own couture house in the early 60s. He quickly gained a reputation for his advanced-looking designs – they were influenced by Balenciaga's severe elegance and architectural approach to cut but they looked younger and more modern. His 1964 autumn collection caused a sensation. It was the most strongly-stated fashion since Dior's 'New Look' of 1947. Dior had been inspired by the romantic costumes of the past; Courreges, in contrast, anticipated the future.

The press revelled in the news value of his bold new concept and Britain's *Queen* magazine (well-respected for its informed fashion coverage) advised its readers:

'You must take Courreges. He's the most terrific phenomenon to hit fashion for years, the heaven of Paris personified. We went to the Collections. We saw. He conquered. We came out dancing in the streets and resolved to bring you for the first time a complete coverage of his sensational clothes because you must take Courreges – and now. He's too good to keep. There's not a moment to lose getting your lucky fashion eye in. Only a few seasons ago Courreges looked years ahead of his time, outrageously outer-planetary. But this time in Paris, ushered in to a background of cosmic jazz, his Collection caused the kind of excitement that

only comes once in a blue moon when the times and fashion meet in a brilliant collision.'

The impact of Courreges's collection was heightened by its presentation in stark, gleaming white showrooms. His models were impressively tall and athletic-looking, suntanned Europeans or glowing black girls.

The geometric lines of the clothes only slightly indicated the figure and, to give them their sculptured shapes, he used firm fabrics – heavy wool crêpe and double- or single-faced gaberdine. For added effect he made complete outfits in dramatic white, bright red or vivid green. Coats, suits, dresses and tunic tops followed the same line, with wide, rounded shoulders, double- and single-breasted, tailored fastenings and stand-away collars. Design details were always precisely proportioned and balanced; to further emphasise the importance of line, collars, seams and pockets were outlined with rows of top-stitching.

City trousers were an important feature of the collection. They were immaculately shaped to give a long, elegant, controlled line and were often cut with centre front seams which opened into short slits at the hem to show boots in a matching colour worn underneath.

Skirts finished several inches above the knee. Although just-above-the-knee hemlines had been worn for several years, particularly in Britain, they were not as short at Courreges's revolutionary minis.

Sixties style personified – the Beatles' wives (from left to right): Patti Harrison, Cynthia Lennon and Maureen Starr. Front: Patti's sister Jenny.

Top left: Black-and-white 'wet-look' PVC raincoats and visor-fronted helmets.

Top right and bottom left: Courreges's forward-looking, sculptured day outfits.

Left and opposite (bottom right):
Paco Rabanne's 'female warrior'
style – blousons and mini-dresses
made from linked-together plastic
discs.

For the first time, skirt lengths were measured as so many inches *above* rather than below the knee. To underline the importance of thigh-high hemlines, Courreges showed specially-designed boots. His famous calf-length, white kid boots, zipped on the inside of the leg and squared-off at the toes, were one of the most copied styles of the mid-60s.

He completed his futuristic look with space-age head-gear: helmet shapes, used for stylised bonnets – unadorned or draped with fabric and tied under the chin – and high-domed caps with rounded peaks or visor fronts.

Paco Rabanne, another new designer hitting the fashion headlines at that time (and still known today for his fragrances), went even further into science-fiction fantasy-dressing and showed his visors and visor-fronted helmets as part of his Amazon-like 'Female Warrior' look, teaming them with tunics, blousons and mini-dresses made from linked-together, metallic-looking plastic discs, designed to simulate chainmail and armour. More commercially accept-able were his fun earrings, also in plastic – shoulder-touching transparent hoops and equally large oval and diamond shapes in black and white, bright red, yellow or two shades of pink.

Still aggressively 60s-modern but less extreme than Paco Rabanne was the young ready-to-wear designers' use of obvious synthetics. Emanuelle Khanh decorated her trouser outfits and mini-dresses with fluorescent plastic cubes. Shiny vinyl was used for Victorire's silver-and-white sleeveless top and mini-skirted action suit, and for Michele Rosier's bright yellow jackets and matching trousers. Housts Sports' zip-fronted boiler suits and matching boots in black 'wet-look' PVC and Rosier's black-and-white raincoats made in the same fabric, were even more striking and an alternative to the growing popularity of leather.

New fashions in leather, influenced by the space-age theme, made the so-called 'kinky leather-gear' of a few years before seem tame. Jackets and blousons were shaped to look like fitted tunics and often had zip and press-stud fasten-ings. They were teamed with matching, tight-fitting pants, boiler suits or miniskirts and knee- or thigh-length, leg-moulding boots.

Honor Blackman as Cathy Gale in the very successful British television series, *The Avengers*, dressed from top to toe in authoritarian fitted leather, a match for any male adversary, played a judo-trained agent who coolly threw strong men over her shoulder at the slightest provocation; and a pretty, youthful-looking Jane Fonda, in her thigh-high leather waders, also made a lasting impression on many men as the heroine in her comic-strip rôle in *Barbarella*.

Although futuristic styling allowed plenty of scope for unisex dressing, its influence on men's fashion was minimal. Tunic-style jackets in leather, wool and cotton, and Pierre Cardin's zip fastenings and zip pockets on collarless tunics, worn over ribbed, rollnecked sweaters and trousers tucked into calf-length leather 'moon boots', were worn by some ultra-fashion-conscious men, but Cardin's pagoda-shaped shoulders, short-length fur coats and thigh-high PVC boots for men rarely got further than the catwalks and publicity pictures.

The 'Space-age Look', like earlier radical fashion changes, was too extreme for most women when it was first introduced. However, once it had been slightly modified and presented in a more wearable form, it became one of the most important trends of the decade. Courreges-style, sharp, clean-cut silhouettes: long, long legs in perfectly-fitting trousers or extrovert boots and minis, all-white outfits, bright, clear colours, silver kid, shiny PVC and crazy plastic jewellery all became part of the 60s interpretation of glamour dressing.

Model-girl types changed to suit the new glamour ideals and stunning black models, like America's 6ft-tall Donyale Luna, were perfect for showing off the new bold shapes and brilliant colours. 'Black is beautiful' was a

The most memorable face and
figure of the 60s – Twiggy – in
David Bond's 1967 'romantic look'
plaid suit and lace ruffles.

popular fashion slogan of the time and helped to boost the
confidence of the black population during the difficult years
of integration.

In dramatic contrast to exotic black looks, equally tall,
cool, athletic Nordic blondes, like Britain's Jill Kennington
and Germany's Verushka, were photographed in exciting
locations as action girls in micro-length T-shirt dresses,
stretch jumpsuits, leather and PVC.

Wacky outfits – tops and skirts or dresses made in colour
blocks of jersey, worn with colour co-ordinating tights and
clashing pop-art style shoes and jewellery – suited the
precocious girly looks of America's Penelope Tree, and
Britain's 16-year-old 'Cockney kid' discovery, Twiggy, with
her adolescent, boyish figure, was just right to portray the
ever more youthful image.

Twiggy appeared even younger than her 16 years when
she started her career – in simple mini-dresses and schoolboy
trouser suits she looked a mere 13 or 14. Fashion had never
known such a childlike ideal. Her poses, skinny, gangly legs
and feet coyly turned inwards, head tilted to one side or shyly
dropped forward, all emphasised extreme youth.

Futuristic designs were often too aggressively stated for
Twiggy's slender looks. Indeed, she was far better suited to
fashion's next move – into the 'Romantic Look'.

The reaction against stark lines started in 1966 when
designers were inspired by the epic movie *Doctor Zhivago*.
Zhivago designs featured immaculately-tailored, calf-length,
brass-buttoned military greatcoats in red or blue-grey, and
Russian-style, side-fastening tunic-blouses in creamy-coloured satin or crêpe, worn with black velvet wrapover skirts
long enough to cover the tops of high boots. Nostalgic,
romantic styles, with a hint of traditional glamour, caught
the public's imagination and made them receptive to the
alternative look in fashion.

Velvet dandy suits became a popular craze of the late
60s for both sexes and ranged from pure fancy dress to

period-costume elegance. The young ultra-fashionable at smart parties often looked as if they were dressed for the stage.

Women with permed blonde curls looked like 'Little Lord Fauntleroys' in frilled-at-the-neck-and-wrist blouses, crushed velvet waistcoats, matching knickerbockers, black tights and buckled shoes. Others dressed as dashing panto-mime principal boys in flared, embroidered velvet jackets, lace ruffled shirts, wide, ornately-buckled belts and tight velvet trousers tucked into just-above-the-knee suede boots.

More coolly stylish was the elegant Mississippi gambler look – hair tied back in a bow, tailored black velvet satin-revered suits, satin waistcoats, silk cravats and slim trousers flaring over high-heeled, patent leather boots.

Fashionable men were just as flamboyantly dressed. Young males with long, floppy hair, sideboards and shaped beards, wearing floaty scarves and satin-piped velvet suits looked like 19th-century poets and painters; and clean-shaven, slim, Renaissance-style youths were even more period costumed. They sported shoulder-length pageboy bobs or girlish curls, wide-sleeved, open-necked, printed velvet shirts fastened with cross-lacing, and jewel-coloured velvet trousers and long boots. They could have been potential Romeos looking for their Juliets, or the latest trendily-dressed pop star sensation.

Idolised pop groups had led the way in fashion from the sharp-tailored 'mod' styles of the early 60s to the sexy fantasy-dressing of the later part of the decade. Lead singers outrageously camped-up their performances in figure-hugging, large-collared shirt-blouses and hip-constraining, flared leather or satin jeans, belted just below the waist with rows of silver or gold chains.

Mick Jagger, dressed in skintight satin, shirt open to the waist, epitomised the new, raunchy male image as he sang, shouted and yelled one of the Rolling Stones' greatest hits '(Can't Get No) Satisfaction'.

Above: The 'goldfinger' mini-skirted disco dress.

Left: Action girls in minimal shiny black shift-dresses.

Right: Evening silhouettes were less contrived in shape, like this marvellously sequinned Cardin sheath.

The fun of putting together individual styles of theatrical costume dressing offered plenty of scope for invention and for mixing clothes from earlier periods with the 60s styles. There was a whole range of popular mixes. Boys wore faded, gold-braided hussars' tunics with their basic flared blue jeans; leather aviators' jackets with crushed velvet and cowboy boots; pre-Second World War, long tweed overcoats and battered leather trenchcoats went over skinny ribbed T-shirts and necklaces, or printed voile shirts and silk scarves; trousers were tucked into riding boots – there were no rules about what went with what. 'Doing your own thing' was a popular expression of the time and style-conscious young men enjoyed presenting their own versions of pop-star glamour.

Girls were just as inventive. Ankle-length maxi-coats and Isadora Duncan-style flowing scarves were worn with sculptured gaberdine mini-dresses, black tights and calf-length, high-laced Edwardian boots. Late-30s silver fox capes went over scoop-necked T-shirts and jeans were tucked into patchwork suede boots. Braided, country-peasant hair-styles went with 30s-style pyjama tops and trousers, snake-skin waistcoats and 40s wedge heels. The permutations were endless for self-indulgent, fantasy dressing.

The style of advanced retail outlets changed to provide the right setting for more romantic looking clothes. One of the most successful in capturing the new mood was retailer Barbara Hulanicki with her London 'Biba' shops (named after her sister). The beautiful Barbara had become well-known and admired for her delightful fashion drawings in the early 60s. Her great feeling for fashion gave the clothes she drew an even more stylish look than they often deserved and made it clear that she had the potential for a greater commitment to the fashion world.

In the mid-60s she started to produce her own range of inexpensive young clothes and opened her first boutique in Kensington. Her early designs were based on a very simple,

feathers. Fox furs, feather boas and soft, pull-on hats were randomly draped over chairs and tables as creating the right background was considered the greatest aid to selling. All in all it was a very different approach to today's emphasis on the importance of hard sell and the commercially-calculated use of every inch of floor space.

Barbara Hulanicki promoted softer looks towards the end of the 60s and, although her clothes were newly made, they had a slightly retro 'un-new' look. She made her designs in rather faded colours – greys, purples, lilacs and dusty pinks and blues. Twenties' fabrics, such as crêpe and jersey, were used for dressmaker-style suits and dresses with draped bodices and gathered sleeves.

Make-up also softened to suit the new fashions and the revamping of earlier glamour ideals. False eyelashes were still popular but slightly less obvious; eye make-up and lipstick were often in tinted peach colours, brown and grey tones. Blushers were used to emphasise cheekbones and make young faces look more mysterious and worldly. Meanwhile, hair was waved into pre-Raphaelite curls or styled into long 30s and 40s movie-star bobs.

Amongst the seemingly endless flow of British designers gaining recognition for their individual style was Ossie Clarke. Originally from the north of England, he was a student at Manchester College of Art before gaining a place at the Fashion School at the Royal College of Art during its vintage years under Janey Ironside. Indeed, he became one of her most outstanding students. His designs, with their clever, inventive cut and use of unusual fabrics, were more exclusive than those of Biba or Mary Quant and his clothes were worn by women renowned for their dress sense, including Mick Jagger's ultra-chic, glamorous first wife, Bianca. Ossie was always advanced in his ideas and was one of the first to launch flatteringly-cut maxi-coats, soft blouses and midi-length skirts. He was especially well-known for his flowing dresses and tops, using textile designer Celia

narrow-shouldered T-shirt shape. She believed that if a woman looked narrow at the top, as in the unemphasised body silhouette of the 60s, she would look narrower all the way down. Her concept suited the waif-like Twiggy ideal and girls flocked to buy Biba designs.

It was another lightning success story of an era when the creative young seemed to lead charmed lives. Biba expanded into ever bigger and more interesting shops. They were darker looking than other stores and boutiques; clothes were hooked on Edwardian bentwood coatstands; potted palms were placed at the foot of stairs and in corners and parts of the shops were decorated with coloured ostrich

Opposite: Italian menswear at the end of the 60s — cravats instead of ties, worn with stylised suits and elegant ankle boots.

Left: Wide culottes were a fashionable alternative to midi- and maxi-length skirts.

Birtwell's lovely prints.

Not all young people were happy with the free-wheeling pop-age way of life, however. They rejected the growing materialism and protested against the condoning of aggressive military action in many parts of the world, particularly the tragic war in Vietnam. They wanted to evolve alternative lifestyles and campaigned for an international brotherhood – 'Love and Peace' was the popular slogan. Huge gatherings of the like-minded, 'love-ins', as they were called, were organised in the States and Europe. Some formed themselves into communes while many went further into escapism. Drug-taking increased alarmingly

and others turned to mysticism, cults and Eastern religions. The new attitudes were reflected in dress; the 'Hippie Look' became a major fashion influence of the late 60s and early 70s.

Both sexes grew their hair to shoulder-length or longer, left it loose and lank, permed it into afro-style 'freak-outs' or, if it was naturally wavy, it was allowed to fall in unarranged curls. Narrow, beaded headbands or printed scarves were sometimes worn across the forehead and fastened at the back. For added effect, some men grew shaggy 'back to nature' beards and moustaches while girls wore flowers in their long hair, and both sexes handed out flowers as a greeting to friends and strangers alike. Although dreamy facial expressions were cultivated, many girls continued to wear 60s-style eye-make-up. Plenty of inexpensive ethnic jewellery was worn by male and female hippies alike; rows of beads hung round necks, bracelets jangled at the wrists and ankles and numerous rings were worn on the fingers of both hands.

Jewellery accessorised traditional Asian cheesecloth shirts and overblouses embroidered with flowers and beads; they were often teamed with Eastern-style tunics and waistcoats and, although the look was sometimes completed with baggy Asian trousers, most hippie men preferred to wear their Western denim or velvet jeans. In the winter, practical and stylish plain or patterned sheepskin-lined afghan jackets were added.

Some went further into authentic Asian dressing and wore floor-length kaftans, edged with braiding and embroidery. (In fact, kaftans for women, with their figure-covering, triangular shape made in a wide range of Eastern and Western fabrics, soon became an established mainstream fashion.) They were usually worn indoors, but some exhibitionist hippies also wore them for walks along city streets and, despite the obvious hazards, they were frequently barefoot beneath their decorative anklets.

Hippie dress was undoubtedly worn by some young people as a sincere expression of their philosophy on life. To many more it was just another fun fashion craze; the term 'hippie' was used to describe a wide range of clothes inspired by other cultures and most fashion-conscious people had at least some ethnic influences in their wardrobes.

The entertainment world commercialised the latest trend. The successful musical *Hair* with its hit song, 'Dawning of the Age of Aquarius', and daring presentation of a nude cast on stage, made show business history as the first hippie musical. Sonny and Cher, ethnically dressed, had great success with their song 'I Got You Babe' and the Beatles received considerable publicity for their pursuit of more spiritual values. They found themselves an Asian guru and adopted more hippie styles of dress with longer, less groomed hairstyles, loose, patterned shirts and embroidered waistcoats. Their later songs, with social messages and deeper meanings, reflected their changed attitudes.

Prestige designers were also influenced by social changes and cult fashions. St Laurent cleverly upmarketed some of the trends with the use of refined cut and expensive couture fabrics. His chic hippie dresses in rich-coloured patchwork prints or shimmering gold, sari-like patterned fabrics, some worn with loosely-cut matching trousers, accessorised with beautiful scarves and colour toning beads, were well received by his establishment-minded clientele; they saw them as a glamorous, younger fashion and a pretty, feminine alternative to more conventional outfits.

Britain's well-liked, talented, ex-Royal College of Art student, Bill Gibb, (sadly to die in his 40s), launched his highly individual interpretation of ethnic designs at the end of the 60s. Some of them were inspired by his Scottish roots and his country background. He mixed unexpected, unusual fabrics together to great effect – tartan jackets and trousers were trimmed with contrasting smaller checks, loose, smock-backed tartan coats had deep edgings of fringed Fair Isle knit, and long, pleated check skirts were cut with inserted bands of country-style prints. The same prints were used for collarless, big-sleeved blouses, topped with handknitted, patterned waistcoats, fastened with crosslacing.

The knitwear in Bill's collections was usually designed by Kaffe Fasset whose inventiveness and artistry of patterns and colourings soon brought him recognition in his own right. Within a few years he became a well-respected authority on creative knitwear and his colourful, instructive books have been an inspiration to many home knitters.

Chelsea's Kings Road on Saturdays in the late 60s was a famous spectacle of stylish looks. Visitors from all over the

Top: Long skirts and artistic prints were important fashion trends of 1970.

Above (middle pic): Yves St Laurent's glamorous theatrical costume look for men.

Bottom left: British designer Bill Gibb with one of his stunning ethnic designs.

Above: The high-fashion version of the popular Afghan and Asian influences.

world came to watch the passing show of hippies, romantic period costume, leather-gear and space-age fashions. London's international image had completely changed within ten years, from a city of conservative, classic elegance to the home of way-out fantasy-dressing.

It was inevitable that there would be a reaction against the anti-materialistic trends and it came in the form of a new, brash 'pop-age' look – 'glam rock' – which was launched in the early 70s. It was very different from earlier ideals of glamour in fashion. Male images were at the forefront of the trend and pop stars, like Marc Bolan, Gary Glitter, David Bowie and Elton John, presented it in its most extreme form. Heads looked large, a mass of permed curls, frizzed freak-outs or long, cut-and-styled helmet-shapes, dyed solid black highlighted with streaks of bright colour and sometimes dotted with glitter. Their faces were more made-up than those of many of the female entertainers, with a liberal use of eyeliner, blusher and even lipgloss!

Skinny tank tops worn without shirts were hung with chains, fancy necklaces and jewelled crosses (sometimes all at once). Tight, just-below the-waist blousons and matching trousers were made in satin or leather often in two contrasting colours. Leg interest was highlighted with trousers tucked into knee-length zippered boots with high heels and platform soles. Gary Glitter's sensational high-camp, silver kid outfits included his famous rock 'n' roll silver platform boots; Elton John wore even higher platforms and David Bowie, who was equally well-known for his footwear, appeared in platform-soled, wedge-heeled shoes covered in glittering multi-coloured sequins.

Platform soles were added to all kinds of male and female footwear to such an extent that, for a few years, it was difficult to find fashionable styles without some kind of elevated lift. Women's shoe designs ranged from sophisticated, Hollywood 40s styles (high- or wedge-heeled, peep-toed, sling-back platforms, in shiny red or black patent), to

Male images, like that of pop star Marc Bolan, were in the forefront of the new trend of the early 70s – 'glam rock'.

wilder 70s pop-age versions with multi-coloured double- and even treble-decker wedge platforms.

High boots had become everyday classics, habitually worn by many men and women. Bought as frequently as shoes, their colours, shapes and design details were changed or revised each season. The basic line for both sexes was leg-shaped and zippered, with round toes, platforms and raised heels. Black leather, as always, was the most commercial, but coloured suedes and reptile skin effects were also popular. Leg and heel heights were generally higher for women than for men and, although wedges were put on some men's boot designs, they were much more popular with women, particularly with eye-catching contrasts, such as red wedges on black patent leather boots, and beige heels with navy or red.

The shock value of the miniskirt waned in the late 60s and longer lengths – to-the-calf midis and ankle-length maxis – were worn as alternatives. In 1970 long skirts were widely promoted and the mini's day was declared over. (*Vogue* went as far as proudly proclaiming its September issue 'Mini Free!') The public was unconvinced; adding length to existing silhouettes often looked dull and aging. It was too soon for such a decisive change and the arrival of glam rock put the long look on hold as leg show went on in a new form.

Hot pants, tight figure-revealing shorts – shorter than minis – worn for nearly all occasions, were the new sensation and, in an era used to fashion shocks, shorts-wearing girls with the right shape still managed to make quite an impression. They wore their tailored, city hot pants with fitted, long-collared blouses, skinny-rib tank tops, fringed shoulder bags, coloured tights and platform shoes or boots. In the winter, fun fur mini-coats (imitation furs dyed in bright colours), shaped cardigans and long scarves were added. For leisure-wear the new shorts were worn with fancy-patterned, waist-length, clinging sweaters and tight

Bis
and shoes used on
on showing the use made
and glitter to glamorise
products. Wellington
med into space wear for
7 with silver paint.
boot decorated with
worn by Dick Emery.
Leather shoe worn by
Clark. Lurex fabric shoe
silver stars glued on
by Polly James in The
Dish.

T-shirts, and disco girls loved showing off their figures and dancing skills in satin or velvet hot pants.

The early 70s option to shorts were flares that were wider than before. Trousers fitting tightly to the knees flared into bell-bottom fullness, helped to look even more elongated and exaggerated by built-up footwear. It was a unisex shape and one of the most commercially successful styled trouser fashions of the pop age.

Couture designers had by now become used to influences from street fashion. St Laurent was one of the most receptive and followed his couture versions of hippie and romantic looks with the very slick and sophisticated adaptation of glam rock.

This included his expertly-tailored, padded-shouldered satin blazer jackets; beautifully-made, quilted-velvet, multi-zipped blousons (accessorised with diamanté stars and crescent-shaped clips); superbly-cut women's shorts, and bulky-shouldered fun furs dyed in dazzling reds, blues and greens. Along with his more delicate, ankle-strapped, sling-backed, platform-soled, sexy women's shoes, sleek, strap-fastened jodhpur boots for men and his range of fragrances for both sexes all became hallmarks of the chic, expensively dressed young international set. Yves St Laurent was at the peak of his fame as the style leader of the 'Beautiful People'.

His women's clothes had a look of the 40s and were at their best on women with an aura of traditional film-star glamour. France's classically beautiful actress, Catherine Deneuve (married for a while in the 60s to the famous photographer, David Bailey), was perfect for the style and has remained one of St Laurent's most loyal and prestigious clients up to the present day.

The predominance of radical new attitudes towards fashion, which had gathered such momentum in the 60s, had led to young men and women dressing more and more alike. Their hairstyles, the cut of their jackets and trousers, the shape of their knitwear and footwear were all very similar.

Left: The knitted maxi-coat over 'matching' sweater and hot pants.

Far left (top): Hot pants with 'pop art' accessories.

Far left (bottom): Outrageous, glittery rock-'n'-roll platform-soled boots were popular with both sexes.

Even styles in jewellery and make-up appeared to be converging and unisex fashion seemed to be set as an irreversible trend. With glam rock – the penultimate pop-age look – the trend had unexpectedly peaked.

More serious times are always reflected in more subdued fashions. In the mid-1970s, after nearly 20 years of lighthearted young fashions, a sobering change of mood began to set in.

The disruptive Middle East war in the autumn of 1973 proved to be a watershed. In the following year oil prices quadrupled, inflation climbed rapidly and world trade went

Above: Revived elegance – the scarved neckline, tailored trouser-suit and long topcoat.

into recession. International confidence was shaken and, although parts of the world managed to absorb the setbacks and resume growth, problems once thought of as belonging to the past resurfaced. Economic decline, unemployment and financial uncertainty returned and persisted.

Fashion changed with the times and became more divisive. With reduced spending power amongst many of the young, the scope for pop-age-style crazes diminished and anti-fashion attitudes began to develop. In contrast, the prosperous, new establishment generation, then settling into their 30s, adopted more expensive, casually sophisticated designs – updated classics and influences from glamour's golden age were revived.

It was a parallel development to the changes at the end of the 1920s when the Bright Young Things, no longer so young, had welcomed the introduction of the more mature, flattering styles of the early 30s.

Many women's fashions of the mid-70s had a look of the 1930s. Heads were neater, with softly-styled bobs and more controlled-looking perms; ladylike hats with dipping brims were sometimes worn. Sophisticated make-up was no longer aimed so exclusively at the experimental young and there was less dramatic emphasis on the eyes. The accent was placed on facial colouring, with blushers widely used and the well-made-up mouth, outlined and lip-glossed, an important feature.

Clothes were still easy-fitting but becoming more shape-conscious, with sharper-shouldered jackets and dresses that showed the curves of the breasts and waist. Skirts were much longer and fuller and mid-calf hemlines finally took over as the predominant fashion length.

Trouser wearing was more popular than ever. Flares modified and often gave way to a mannish line influenced by the 30s and 40s. Still close-fitting over the seat, the revised shape had front pleats and straight, wider-cut legs. Trouser suits in smooth menswear fabrics – grey flannel, neat checks

and city stripes — with sharply-tailored pants and immacu-
lately-cut jackets were popular. Silk blouses were topped
with calf-length fur or cloth coats, or military-style trench
coats, preferably all by Yves St Laurent. Worn by lookalike
blonde-bobbed Catherine Deneuves, in wide-rimmed, tinted
sunglasses, a popular glamour image of a chic, international-
set woman was formed.

Equally mannish styles had been worn by the film stars
40 years earlier, when Greta Garbo, Marlene Dietrich and
Katharine Hepburn had conveyed to great effect the sex
appeal of a feminine woman wearing masculine clothes.

Many British designers seemed less at home with the
more subdued fashions of the late 70s but there were
exceptions. Among them were Jean Muir (her masterly
understatement was even more successful) and ready-to-
wear designers, Janice Wainwright, John Bates and Roland
Klein, with their sophisticated styles reflecting the changing
mood. London remained an important and established part
of the international fashion scene but its exuberant, youthful
confidence waned and Paris, Milan and New York, perhaps
always more traditional at heart, took the fashion lead.

The re-established supreme authority of Paris was
achieved through the talents of its leading ready-to-wear
designers. Their chic 'city casual' look and range of clothes
that could be worn for many occasions suited the busy, more
egalitarian way of life far better than the remote world of
haute couture.

St Laurent, the top name of the mid-70s, successfully
bridged the two fashion worlds. He retained the prestige of
his couture house, where he could experiment with new
lines, show beautiful, extravagant clothes and cater for his
exclusive, international clientele, and at the same time he
expanded and developed his 'Rive Gauche' ready-to-wear
collections.

St Laurent shops, designed and fitted out to exact
specifications, opened in major cities and fashionable resorts

Overleaf (right): The layered look
of the mid-70s.

Overleaf (left): Pinky mauve
knitted outfit designed by Sonia
Rykiel.

Above: Top model Marie Helvin
wearing Yves St Laurent's
interpretation of ethnic dressing.

all over the world. They sold an extensive range of his womenswear and fragrances, and also his newly important menswear. His exquisite men's clothes, with distinct seasonal changes of line, fabrics and colours, were for a while as trendsetting as his women's and received considerable publicity. To emphasise their glamour appeal they were often photographed on slim, good-looking young actors, including Austrian star Helmut Berger, admired for his Adonis-like physique and striking blond looks. He was impressively described at the time as 'the most beautiful man in the world'.

Later, as St Laurent became even more commercially successful, his name was put on a much wider range of more basic fashion items, available in many mid-level boutiques and departmental stores. Some of his fickle fashion devotees sensed a loss of exclusivity, became less committed to the St Laurent label and turned their attention to other up-and-coming designers – Karl Lagerfeld, Sonia Rykiel and Kenzo were the exciting new fashion discoveries of the time.

Karl Lagerfeld, still such an important fashion influence today, became internationally known with his collections for Chloe and the Chloe shops. He has always had an intuitive sense of fashion timing, designing clothes with the exact look women wanted to wear at any given time, rather than presenting them with controversial new concepts. The Germanic clarity of his precise silhouettes, design details and colours have given women a status-conscious glamour look that has had worldwide appeal, particularly the 'Lagerfelding' of the Chanel image during the 80s.

Although never well-known for his menswear, Lagerfeld's own very distinct image, with his simple pony-tail hairstyle, has been widely copied and has become almost a caricature feature of men in the design and media world.

Sonia Rykiel, like other talented female designers (especially Chanel), offered something extra in her style concept, a subtle quality that male designers could not provide – the feminine instinct of knowing what pleases women in the clothes they wear and the image they present. Sonia looked enviably good in her own designs, presenting a perfected personal style, but also one to which women could relate.

Her clothes were soft, feminine, beautifully-coloured and guaranteed to flatter. A subtle, easy-to-wear line with jersey wraps and capes; lean, gently-pleated or lightly-gathered, low calf-length jersey skirts; plain and striped, body-clinging dresses or sweaters in cashmere, angora or lambswool; long mohair and wool cardigan jackets teamed with matching knitted scarves. Her outfits were superbly colour toned or colour co-ordinated and ranged from the elegant neutrals – classic cream, ivory, navy and black – to the shell colours – pinky beige, oyster shades, pearl, blue-greys and the soft toned brights – iris blue, turquoise and fuchsia pink.

Kenzo was the first of many Japanese designers to have a strong influence on Paris fashion. His designing (such a well-respected part of the classic establishment Paris ready-to-wear today) was refreshingly inventive when it first became famous in the mid-70s. His early designs – braided wool jackets worn with swirling, calf-length printed skirts over high-heeled boots; loose-fitting, high-waisted, embroidered smock dresses; baggy boilersuits and oversized sweaters worn as tunics or mini-dresses with leg warmers – were all the novel ideas of the young Kenzo, destined to become widely adopted mainstream fashions of the late 70s.

Italy, well-known for directional menswear since the 50s, had steadily built up its reputation for women's designs. In the 70s it really came into its own and, by the end of the decade, Milan was second only to Paris as an international fashion centre.

Valentino, a favourite designer of image-conscious, rich and famous women all over the world for several decades (an Italian equivalent to France's Pierre Balmain with his *jolie madame* philosophy), has always been Italy's glamour traditionalist.

He continued to produce his style of opulent, womanly clothes in rich fabrics, lavishly trimmed with fur and embellished with embroidery, throughout the youth cults, street fashions and under-played chic of the late 70s. His reputation was boosted and reached a new peak in the designer 80s, when fashion came his way and all-out glamour and affluent power-dressing became such an admired ideal.

The 70s was an exciting decade for knitwear designers. None were more creative than the Italians and the Missoni family's collections were outstanding.

The Missonis' inventive use of yarns — varying mixes of linen, cotton and silk, lambswool, mohair, boucle, alpaca and chenille – combined with the artistry of their colourings, produced stunning results that took knitwear to the forefront of high fashion for the first time.

Missoni combined delicate neutrals and pastels for spring and summer – creamy beiges, ivory, pearl grey, pale shades of gold and turquoise; for autumn and winter Italian Renaissance shades were used – wine reds with forest greens and smoky blues, yellow golds with rusty orange and charcoal grey.

The creativity of using unusual yarns and well-chosen colours was clearly shown when they were knitted into subtle stripes, patchwork effects and patterns that looked like tapestries. The fabrics were knitted or sewn into hats, scarves, sweaters, cardigans, dresses and coats. To make complete outfits they were carefully co-ordinated with trousers and skirts made in plain jersey or woven fabrics and, for added effect, dashing capes in woven, colour-toning blanket checks were sometimes added.

The unique Missoni style has remained well-known up to the present day. Their designs are always interesting but the scope for innovation within their concept has inevitably been limited and the excitement of their earlier vintage collections difficult to maintain.

Although very different to the receptive atmosphere of 'swinging London' as the centre for experimental, irreverent pop-age fashion in the 60s, Milan's ultra-style-conscious but more conformist interpretation of fashion suited the grown-up mood which developed during the 1970s and the city became the Mecca for aspiring talent. International buyers promoted Italian designers as they had British ones ten years earlier. Every season new names were enthusiastically reported by the world's fashion press, including two big stars of the future – Gianni Versace and Giorgio Armani.

America's astute buyers ensured that all the latest trends and newsworthy European designers were available in the States. A few of their own well-respected designers, in particular Bill Blass, Halston and Geoffrey Beene, were known internationally. Generally, however, American stylists concentrated on the substantial home market.

Apart from film and TV stars' looks, and Western and hippie-style fads, the US had been less of an influence on world fashion during the pop-age years, and a directional American look remained in eclipse until the late 70s.

The independent-spirited, young, urban American women had been less comfortable than many of their European counterparts with the 'naughty girl' fashion images of the 60s. Although women at the time were supposed to be enjoying a greater sense of liberation, they were often portrayed by the media in a sexist way. They were shown as the essential complementary accessory to the cool, stylishly confident male; his 'doll' or 'bird', clinging to his arm, peeping over his shoulder or sitting admiringly at his feet, provocatively dressed to turn him on and looking sexually available.

Feminism gathered strength in the States and also affected women's attitudes in other parts of the world. By the end of the decade, the body- and health-conscious, competitive young woman, dressed for self-esteem, had emerged.

American designers were the first to dress the new ideal and soon became an international influence. *Vogue* promoted the 'Great American Look' and informed its readers:

The Americans make clothes that race along with their whole health and beauty kick. They're marvellous, adaptable, simple, chic. Suedes and leathers cutting a fine swathe, silks and satins, neutral shades, plain and perfect for dressing up or down. Calvin Klein is master of the look.

Calvin Klein, with his film-star good looks, produced refreshingly simple, easy-to-wear, desirable clothes: slightly padded-shouldered, straight-cut jackets over draped or camisole tops; slim, wrapover, knee-length skirts and gently-tapered trousers – all in sensuous fabrics and flattering colours, like caramel, creamy beige, pale coffee with white or a flash of bright colour – a tomato-red linen blazer or a jade-green silk T-shirt. To add an ultra-feminine touch to his spring 1979 collection, he showed high-heeled, strappy mules with many of his outfits.

The look of the late-20th-century American woman was most strongly conveyed in the glitzy, glossy soap operas. *Dallas* and *Dallas* women were appearing on more and more TV screens worldwide; Sue-Ellen's shoulders were visibly widening and the stage was being set for the power-dressed 80s.

The male glamour image also matured during the 70s. Britain's latest pop star idol, Bryan Ferry, a young sophisticate in smooth designer suits and classic jackets in soft leather, Robert Redford's all-American golden-boy looks (never too fashionably dressed, but always appropriately turned out as action man, sportsman or thinking man), and Richard Gere's moody, dark looks in American casuals or immaculate Armani clothes for *American Gigolo*, were all role models for the smart new woman's ideal man.

The widening chasm between the haves and the have-nots had become much more apparent by the second half of the 70s. Many of the less affluent young appeared anti-fashion in their attitude towards clothes. Egalitarian, habitual jeans-wearing by both sexes had become as much a uniform of the Western world as the Mao Tse-Tung cotton tunics in regimented communist China.

Some young men in the US and Europe reacted against the softer male looks of the romantic, hippie and glam rock cults, adopted a more macho, aggressive style and wore army-type clothes. Their outfits consisted of khaki or camouflage US military caps, military shirts with original or fake badges and stripes on the sleeves and tight khaki jeans or authentic combat trousers.

In Britain, a new brutal-looking street style caught on – the skinhead look. Working-class boys cropped and shaved their hair more severely than any army recruit, wore plain, vest-like tops, dull, collarless shirts and baggy-seated trousers or jeans hitched-up high with braces to show heavy, laced working boots. Skinheads received a great deal of unfavourable publicity, were associated with mindless aggression and were reputed to be full of 'aggro', always looking for trouble. Many young men simply liked to identify with the tough macho style. It was a most unglamorous cult style and was the forerunner of an even more controversial anti-fashion, the last pop-age look to be a major international influence on the way people dressed – punk rock.

Few styles have been so vehemently condemned. To many people, punk fashions were deliberately ugly and made the wearer unnecessarily unattractive. It is hard to find any comparable attitude towards appearance in the history of costume. The closest parallel must be that of certain primitive jungle tribes, belligerent witch doctors and Red Indian braves who made themselves look frighteningly ferocious as a weapon of intimidation. Few punks actually

Above: The striking Zandra Rhodes in her North American Indian look.

Left: Two of Zandra's outfits from her glamorised punk collection.

Right: Debbie Harry, lead singer with chart-topping band Blondie, took her inspiration for style from Marilyn Monroe.

Striking Bill Gibb design oozing 70s style.

wanted to frighten or intimidate but they did want to be noticed and London 'punk-spotting' became a popular preoccupation. The regular group of punks that gathered in Chelsea's King's Road often charged a fee to be photographed with, and by, fascinated tourists, anxious to record the new phenomenon.

Punks, male and female, cut their hair short and spiky all over, or shaved their heads apart from a high-standing tuft of hair running from front to back over the head – the 'Mohican'. Hair was dyed startling colours – fluorescent orange, pink, blue or green (sometimes several strong colours were used on the same head to give a striped or patchwork effect). Faces were often pale chalk-white with blackened eye sockets or highlights of bright colours were round the eyes and on the cheeks. The area round just one eye was sometimes made-up in multi-coloured, geometric shapes and some of the most outrageous punks had safety pins through their noses and/or ears. Clothes were usually all black or black teamed with a strong colour (pink was a favourite), ocelot prints or bright red Royal Stuart tartan.

Loose T-shirts had ink-like blobs or messages and slogans like 'Destroy' printed on them. Jackets and trousers were in matt or sheen cotton, occasionally rubber, leather, or leather-look fabrics like PVC. So-called 'bondage trousers' were joined together at the back with loose, dangling straps; lengths finished well above the ankle to show brightly coloured socks and high-laced, black leather or rubber combat boots.

Both sexes wore similar styles but some girls wore miniskirts with bright-coloured footless tights and pointed-toe, stiletto-heel court shoes. Boys and girls accessorised their outfits with black leather studded wristbands and dog collars, while some punks took exhibitionism and sado-masochistic connotations even further and led one another on chain leads which they had clipped to their dog collars.

Was punk as far away from glamour in fashion as it is possible to get or simply a revolt against long-accepted standards of beauty and style? Punks may not have used the word 'glamour' but they no doubt thought an exceptionally striking, well-turned-out punk, male or female, in full regalia, to be their equivalent of glamorous. Punk had made a big enough impression for *Vogue* to do a feature on the new trend in 1977.

New fashions are always overstated and the young generation often want to shock and outrage their elders with wildly unconventional styles. For those in older age groups it was certainly difficult to understand the appeal of punk. However, during the next few years fashion designers refined and adapted some of the original ideas and many acceptable fashions at the end of the 70s and during the early 80s were, in fact, punk-inspired.

By the close of the 70s, style had become more divisive than it had been for decades. Jeans and trainers, tracksuits, boilersuits and bondage punk were a far cry from glamour's golden age or the fantasy run of the recent past. Fashion had sunk to a low point.

For the affluent, more elitist styles were on offer – colourful, specifically-designed sportswear for the body-conscious, body-developed, social sportswoman and man. Designer, status-symbol menswear, and a stronger silhouette for women with wider shoulders, shaped waists and shorter, straighter skirts all held appeal. Glamour dressing that proclaimed a high price tag was already indicating the character of the next decade.

The Glamour Renaissance

Glamour Updated

The 80s and early 90s

SECTION THREE Why are yesterday's fashions, which were once admired and thought so right, always ridiculed and rubbished a decade or so later?

Any fashion loses its appeal when it has been overplayed, become over-familiar and progressively down-marketed. James Laver, the revered fashion historian, in his book *Taste and Fashion*, first published over 50 years ago, maintained that when a particular style has lost favour, distance in time is required before it can be extolled once again. He went as far as indicating an approximate timescale for an item's rehabilitation: first it goes through an unpopular phase of about 20 years duration, when it is considered hideous and ridiculous; after 30 years it becomes interesting and amusing; after 40 – quaint; over 50 years later it is safely 'period costume' and is often considered 'romantic'.

Despite the social upheavals of the last half-century, which have been reflected in many new concepts and attitudes towards fashion, James Laver's theory still holds good in the 1990s. Today, the styles of the 80s – along with the whole character of the decade – are already being discredited. *Vogue*, in its spring 1992 fashion reports, puts down the 80s with the following comments: 'Tired leggings, obsessional black'; 'caricatures of girlishness, glitziness and exaggerated sexiness that so often assailed us'; and goes on to devalue the typical 80s suit – 'you will be forced to laugh, if affectionately, at the memory of the person you were when you wore those wide-shouldered, short-skirted two pieces in "serious" black or "assertive" red.'

The young at the beginning of the 80s – tempered by one recession and facing up to another – re-evaluated style and fashion for their time. There was a well-established market for casual clothes and sportswear, but dressiness and formality, neglected for a generation, began to be revived.

In an ever more competitive world, achievement was all-important and presenting a slick, sharp, business-like appearance was considered essential. Nostalgia for the stylishness of the past portrayed in old movies and recreated

Opposite: Assertive silhouettes with wide shoulders and shorter skirts characterised the power-dressed stylishness of the 80s.

in successful TV series, like Britain's elegant *Edward and Mrs Simpson* and *Brideshead Revisited*, also helped to bring about the reformation of more status-conscious dressing.

Young men and women whose pop-age parents had brought them up in T-shirts and jeans, enjoyed the impact and ego-boost of high-profile 'dressing to impress'. During the day, both sexes had groomed hairstyles and wore well-tailored suits.

Special evening occasions required black tie formality for men and a Cinderella-like change of image for women. The sheer femininity of young women wearing ball dresses with puffed-sleeves, figure-shaped bodices and full, swirling skirts – and the clean-cut, affluent look of young men in evening suits, wing-collared shirts, bow ties and sleek short hair – all had a fresh appeal. The allure of traditional glamour inspired by glamour's golden age had embarked on its comeback.

The Princess of Wales, in the glare of publicity which surrounded her, helped to popularise the trend with her choice of clothes, particularly her big-sleeved, full-skirted, romantic-looking wedding dress, designed by the Emanuels (versions of which were worn by many brides throughout the 80s), and her glamorous evening dresses.

Glossy magazines like *Harper's Bazaar* and *Vogue* revelled in the revival of rich, formal evening wear, and in their important Collection issues, headlined leading pictures with 'Putting on the Style', 'The Power of Positive Slinking' and 'Très Belle Epoque'. There were endless pages featuring exclusive couture evening dresses of stunning designs: St Laurent's huge pink satin bow draped over a long black velvet sheath; his violet-and-gold lace body-clinging dress swathed and sashed in toning blue silk; Ungaro's turn-of-the-century-inspired taffeta outfit, a sleeveless cape worn over a matching puff-sleeved dress, draped into a bustle-backed train, and Givenchy's slender movie-star gown, a long white satin sarong, wrapped over and trimmed with

black feathers and a pearl brooch – high glamour dresses, all catching the new mood of unashamed opulence.

Even some street fashion cults (less important than in previous decades) presented a softer look, particularly the 'New Romantics' with their frilly shirts, sashed waists and knee-breeches.

Rich glamour looks extended from top to toe. Make-up was more strongly stated with skilfully applied blushers and bolder, more dramatic colour for eyes and lips. Professional make-up artists, once confined to filmsets and fashion shoots, were available to the more affluent general public.

Permed hair was still popular but it had become more luxuriant-looking and was often developed into lion's-mane

Above: Princess Diana's style-conscious appearance became more confident and glamorous as the decade progressed.

effects with the help of the re-introduction of back-combing and new drying techniques like 'scrunching' (invented by top hairdresser, Trevor Sorbie). Hair looked fuller but not hard and set; the wide range of mousses and gels on offer provided greater holding power without forfeiting movement and flexibility (a great improvement on the stiff, lacquered hairstyles of the 60s).

Forties-style upswept side-rolls looked sophisticated again, and hair brushed over to one side or arranged in an angled topknot, held in place with brightly coloured hair accessories, were popular with the young. Older women frequently copied the fringe and the winged sides worn by *Dynasty* star, Linda Evans.

Blond streaks and highlighting became extremely popular for both sexes. In fact, it was one of the most widely-used glamour fixes of the 80s. Subtle highlighting certainly helped to liven up unremarkable natural colouring but repeatedly-applied colour soon looked artificial, and as the decade progressed many heads became 'over-blonded' and out of condition.

The return to more considered, dressed-up urban fashions called for glamorous designer hats to complete the look. Although hats still tended to be worn mainly for special occasions, they were a more admired part of the overall fashion picture than they had been for several decades.

The femininity of wearing glamorous hats was redis-

Above: Chart-toppers of the early 80s, Adam and the Ants helped to promote the softer-looking 'New Romantic' style.

Leading pop groups Duran Duran
(top) and Spandau Ballet promoted
'designer' looks and encouraged a
more considered style for men.

covered by older women and enjoyed for the first time by the younger generation. Once again, the Princess of Wales, whose public appearances often required hats, led the trend – particularly amongst the young who, until then, had associated hat-wearing with their mothers and grandmothers.

Styles were inspired by the 30s, 40s, and 50s. Wavy-brimmed, deep-crowned, colonial garden-party hats had a dreamy, romantic appeal. Nostalgia for Hollywood's famous stars, like Bette Davis and Joan Crawford, was shown in sophisticated, side-tilted boater- and saucer-shapes, trimmed with ribbons and sometimes made in two contrasting colours

Flattering, forward-tilted pillboxes decorated with flowers and veiling, or made in velvet with satin bands draped through diamanté buckles, were equally popular. The couture elegance of the early 50s was echoed in dramatic-looking fashion-model styles – black-and-white wide-brimmed shapes worn straight across the forehead, or huge, back-sweeping designs with the front brim turned up off the face and held with a bow or flower.

Fashionable 80s-style dressing for both sexes was based on possessing or striving for the well-developed, well-proportioned body. Skinny was definitely out and figures had to fill out and firm up. The famous models of the decade, like Jerry Hall and Marie Helvin, were less fragile-looking than their predecessors; taller, bigger-built figures suited the strongly-stated silhouettes and curvy fit of the time. Most periods emphasise and sometimes exaggerate one or two features of the female form; the 80s – in keeping with its acquisitive character – accentuated everything at the same time: shoulders, breasts, waists, hips and legs.

Although men's clothes were more conformist and less figure-fitting, they were not designed for 'wimps'. Broad-shouldered, loose-cut, double-breasted suit jackets, roomy leather blousons, long topcoats and pleated pants all demanded to be shown off by tall, athletically-built men who looked as if they were well-muscled under the nonchalant understatement of their Armani classics, or the easy fit of their Levi 501 jeans.

Exercise became more than a fad – it was a part of the modern lifestyle which sometimes verged on the obsessive. In America alone there were reported to be 10 million female joggers and 10,000 female weightlifters! Participation in skiing, riding, tennis, cycling and swimming hit an all-time high. Fitness was an important feature of the corporate profile for men and women, with some companies even installing their own in-house gyms and squash courts. Outside the office, ever-growing numbers attended gyms and dance studios, while jazz dance and aerobics became more than passing crazes and celebrities, like Jane Fonda with her 'workout' books, boosted the exercise preoccupation. Sales of keep-fit videos boomed and personal fitness trainers became the 'thing to have' in wealthy circles.

After a brief pause waiting for the early-80s recession to pass, designers resumed the development of the wide-shouldered silhouettes introduced in the late 70s. Shoulder-pads were soon appearing in every kind of garment from cardigans to ball dresses. Like other dominant fashions it became all-invasive and, by the middle of the decade, it was almost impossible to buy new garments *without* pads.

TV audiences were intrigued as the shoulder lines of *Dallas* star, Linda Gray, and *Dynasty* stars, Linda Evans and Joan Collins, became ever more extended. Unrestricted width at the top was soon recognised as a potential problem for passing through doorways in the normal manner, just as crinoline-size below the waist had been in the 1860s. Shoulder width mercifully peaked in the late 80s, after having beaten Joan Crawford's previous record in the 1940s film *Mildred Pierce* by a couple of centimetres.

The fashions worn in *Dallas* and *Dynasty*: just-out-of-the-salon hairstyles, assertive silhouettes, sarong drapery, fluted peplums and dressy, wedding-style hats, became one of the strongest influences on women's clothes, and to many epitomised the high-gloss of 80s glamour. Joan Collins showed – to the delight of many older women – that you didn't have to be young to be considered glamorous. In fact, many fashions of the mid-80s suited the over-30s age group better than the very young. Although the soaps were clearly influenced by Hollywood 'women's pictures' of the 30s and 40s, the new fantasy world was less about high society and romance, and had more to do with power, control, instant gratification and, above all, flaunting one's wealth.

In 1980, after nearly 70 years of ups and downs, hemlines which had been revised to the decreed correct length at least twice in every decade, were once again in the news, and were shortening to around knee-level. During the first half of the decade, they dipped again – sometimes right down to the low-calf-lengths of the early 20s and 30s. In the mid-80s, hems, like the stock market, were rising, to the knee and above and, by 1987, well-above-the-knee had become the predominant fashion length. Legginess was even more fashionable in the late 80s and early 90s with mini- and microskirts, stretch pants, tights, fancy patterned leggings, lycra cycling shorts and revived hotpants. Unlike earlier periods, however, there were always longer skirt options; in Britain in particular, low-calf became an established favourite. For the first time, most women were less preoccupied about exact hemlines and usually had a variety of lengths in their wardrobe.

Although basic black had never been more popular – particularly with the business-minded young – bold, strong colours were also very much a part of dressed-up glamour looks. Cobalt blue, vibrant mauve, bright fuchsia and guardsman red contrasting with black, and black and white for summer, were some of the most popular fashion colours. Later in the decade, harder-to-wear oranges, yellows and lime greens were promoted.

With legs firmly aboard the glamour bandwagon, the sheer and fancy-patterned stockings, and tights with lacy designs or delicate heel- and side-motifs, favoured by many women, caught the attention of male eyes. Although the practical aspect of tights made them established basics, more women wore stockings and suspenders. Some die-hard feminists of the 70s considered this a betrayal and a capitulation to male chauvinism. Many 80s women, however, were more relaxed about their liberation, and enjoyed the sensual *femme-fatale* appeal of wearing sexy stockings and very feminine lingerie as alternative, fun ways of dressing.

Expensive-looking, slender, high-heeled, almond-toed court shoes in black leather or suede, complemented sheer stockings and were the established city classics of the time, and the hallmark of the power-dressed female executive.

Later, shoe designs became more varied with sling-backed court shoes and strappy, 20s-style, high-heeled evening sandals. Decorative effects were also widely used: bows, embroidery, fancy clips and buckles. Overall, shoes were more colourful – in the summer, bright reds and blues together with updated 30s styles, white with navy or black toe-caps and heels were worn. In the autumn, rich jewel colours, often in suede, were promoted: wine reds, deep purples, inky blues and dark greens.

Boots, so much a part of the 60s and 70s style images, were less fashionable for a few years, but came back strongly in the late 80s as part of the 60s 'pop age' revival. Women's boots of the 80s ranged from neat, ankle-covering laced designs and elastic-sided Chelseas to the always-admired knee-high riding boots and on to thigh-length 'Barbarella' waders in soft leather, shiny black or coloured patent and theatrical-looking, plain or embroidered, brightly-coloured satin.

The 1980s have often been called 'the designer decade'; a concept that was certainly over-used and over-applied. As

Opposite: For many women, the expensively-dressed cast of the glitzy, highly successful American soap *Dynasty* epitomised 80s glamour.

well as clothes, there were designer cars parked outside designer homes, which had designer kitchens with designer food in the fridge, and the alarming increase in drug-taking was often glossed over by describing the illegal substances as 'designer drugs'.

As prosperity increased, fashion boomed and there was plenty of activity amongst the world's dress designers. For all its glitz and glamour, however, styling – with a few exceptions – was predominantly traditional rather than radically creative.

In Britain, Bruce Oldfield produced flattering, desirable, womanly clothes with more than a hint of glamour's 'golden age'. The styles of Jasper Conran (son of Terence Conran, the well-known design entrepreneur) were coolly elegant, often understated and suited a wide range of ages. Even Katharine Hamnett's zippy young designs were often inspired by the pop-age heroes of previous decades. Vivienne Westwood was one of the few well-known designers who kept alive the spirit of controversial, irreverent and experimental fun that had been so much a part of the freewheeling young concepts which had revolutionised and made fashion so exciting in the 1960s.

In Paris, Jean Paul Gaultier was France's most successful new *avant-garde* designer. His fashion shows always included some 'guaranteed to shock' themes which made exciting press reports and wacky newspaper pictures. His extreme outfits were usually backed up with a good selection of more wearable clothes, and he often toned down, modified and adapted his wilder themes for future collections. One of the best examples of this was the 'underwear look' worn as outerwear. Bras on top of other garments, or worn as on-view everyday items, made fashion headlines but were soon assimilated into mainstream trends, and the bustier top became one of the most commercial fashions of the decade.

Paris has always been known for designers with an elegant, cultivated style, masters in the evolution of cut,

understatement and throwaway chic – in the 'pop age' they had often been criticised for being too restrained. In marked contrast, the important Paris designers of the 80s went in for much more showy looks. Bright colours – reds, blues, pinks, yellows and greens – eclipsed the neutrals loved by earlier couturiers and, for added effect, embellishment was often combined with strong colour.

Christian Lacroix was in the forefront of the new trend and made his short-skirted, fitted silhouettes in exciting mixes of colour and design. He teamed one print with

Above and right: Montana's authoritarian line – sharp shoulders and city-smart jodhpurs.

another different one, prints with checks, and sometimes decorated his colourful patterned fabrics with rich-looking embroideries.

Ungaro, already well-known for his use of prints, also promoted more extrovert designs in striking, brightly-coloured florals or abstracts, which he used for his 'rich lady' dresses. Designs with either long-torsoed, strapless, hourglass tops or ruched and swathed bodices with gathered sleeves, were teamed with very short, draped or puffball skirts.

Karl Lagerfeld's revamping of Chanel couture replaced the long-established, underplayed character of the original concept with a much slicker, more obviously-expensive style, aimed at a wider market. He cleverly adapted Chanel's well-known themes – multi-pocketed braided suits, brass buttons, interesting tweeds and white-collared silky blouses – to the commercial tastes of the time. He used the popular primary colours, particularly red or blue with black, and he liberally decorated sharp-shouldered, precise silhouettes and ever-shortening skirts with shiny buttons and chains. It was all a great success and the new 80s Chanel suit became one of the most popular status-symbol styles of the decade.

Chanel shops opened in many more cities and fashionable resorts all over the world, and the same Chanel suits were seen in shops as far apart as Tokyo and Palm Beach, Florida. But would Coco Chanel, arguably the most influential designer of the 20th century, who had promoted the more subtle glamour of understated dressing, have approved of putting her name to such a change of image?

In the late 80s and early 90s, many Paris designers were clearly influenced by the 1960s and some revived the 'pop age' glamour appeal of the science-fiction space-age look. Claude Montana showed simple, mini-length shift dresses, A-line tunic jackets and ultra-short, trapeze-shaped tent coats in bright pinks, oranges and yellows, with matching or contrasting tights. He also re-introduced zips as a style feature for angled fastenings, to close pockets, or purely for decoration.

Thierry Mugler was another designer who had fun bringing back the 60s-modern, futuristic look, although his interpretation was more stagey and tongue-in-cheek. His silhouettes were totally figure-demanding with wide-winged shoulders, moulded bodices, nipped-in waists, micro-lengths and shiny tights or leggings. Some of his wilder outfits looked unadulterated 'comic-book' with hoods, startling wigs and outrageous thigh-length boots edged with wide

Above and far right: Strongly stated looks – curvy designer jackets, minimal skirts and plenty of leg show.

Right: In the middle of the decade, many skirts were still worn calf-length and the flattering sarong style was revived.

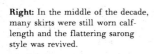

bands of fake fur, all made in bright colours or icy pastel-blue or pink. The audience of buyers and press thoroughly enjoyed his spectacular fashion presentations and some of the styles had a noticeable influence on the mass market.

Wholesale manufacturers, always looking for new trends to commercialise, adapted Montana's and Mugler's 'pop-age' designs and found that their lively, colourful, 60s styles had a fresh appeal to the new generation, too young to remember the original versions.

Milan became even more important as an international fashion centre in the 1980s. Often more restrained than Paris (but always interesting and world famous for its tempting fashion shops and impressively high standard of dressing), the Italian designers are considered the most important alternative source of fashion inspiration, and the Milan Collections are a must for international fashion buyers and the press.

Byblos, with its two talented resident British designers, Alan Cleaver and Keith Varty (both trained at the Fashion School at the Royal College of Art, in London) have produced continually good collections of young, forward-looking, casually-chic women's and men's clothes, and are especially well-known for their colour sense and inventive prints and knitwear.

Kritzia's slightly more strongly stated style has become known for a 'smart international woman' look of slick tailoring, elegant city casuals and feminine dresses. The Kritzia shops, decorated in an understated, 30s-modern style to provide the perfect background for showing off the clothes, have opened in many capital cities.

Valentino, Italy's 'King of Glamour', sometimes known as the Rolls-Royce of fashion, became famous for his dedication to glamorising women. His clothes have all the traditional qualities that only couture and the top ready-to-wear can offer — exclusively made fabrics, expert cut and rich-looking trimmings: furs, fancy braiding and specially-

designed buckles and belts. His evening dresses are famed for their opulence and feature the richest fabrics and the most precious embroideries.

Gianni Versace has steadily built up his reputation as one of the most creative, newsworthy, international designers; although Italian, his style is nearer to Paris with its ability to shock and amuse. Working with his glamorous sister, he was one of the leaders of the sexy, extrovert style that became such a strong trend in the late 80s. He is particularly famous for his men's and women's decorated, sophisticated leather 'rocker' outfits (adored by show business stars), his elaborately embroidered women's dresses, jackets, and daring bustier tops, and for his hot-coloured, widely-copied 'pop age' prints, used for dashing, clingy tops, T-shirt dresses and leggings.

Amongst all the stagey showiness of the 80s and early 90s – the opulent glamour and 'rich lady' retro looks of the first half of the period and the tight fit, titillation, body show, vivid colours and glittering embellishments of the later years – Giorgio Armani has stood out as the most influential contemporary designer who has not abandoned elegance, flattering understatement and the subtle evolution of cut that had been the hallmarks of earlier great designers such as Chanel, Vionnet, Molyneux and Balenciaga.

Above: Montana's interpretation of two classic looks – draped creamy-beige evening dresses and 'little black dresses' trimmed with chiffon.

The bold combination of black and white – always effective – suited fashion's confident mood in 1987.

Armani's style has much in common with Chanel's, and he might be the one designer she would have approved of for keeping alive so much of her own fashion philosophy. Armani, like Chanel, believes in perfected cut that flatters the form but at the same time gives a youthful, unrestricted fit. He loves soft, neutral colours; his exquisite palette of tinted beiges and greys, bluey-greens, smokey-blues, hints of khaki, sun-baked earth colours and cool, unsugary pastels are so well-known that 'Armani colours' like 'Schiaparelli shocking pink' have become a part of the fashion vocabulary.

Although Armani clothes are often considered modern high-fashion classics, they have always been very directional – Armani was one of the first designers to promote big shoulders, collarless jackets, short skirts, camisole tops, sarong drapery and roomy pleated pants. Amongst the great designers of the 20th century, he is probably unique for being equally well-known, or even more famous, for his glamorous menswear which, to many people, is simply the ultimate in stylishness.

Fashions for men and women in the 80s generally became more separated than at any time since the 50s. The serious business of making money demanded a conformist businessman-like appearance and city whizz kids dressed the part with slick, gelled short hair, immaculate shirts and ties, designer suits (sometimes with braces attached to their pleated pants) and polished, conventional shoes. There was no male equivalent to women's fashion's sexy body show, as there had been in the 'pop age'. Even men's casual clothes were more played down; leather blousons had become a classic, sports jackets and blazers were revived and easier fitting jeans became fashionable. More obvious showing off of the male body had to be reserved for the serious sportsman in his functional sports gear. Cycling, like jogging, had become a part of some men's regular programme of keeping fit, and body-gripping stretch-lycra shorts certainly drew attention to male contours.

Although Armani's menswear concept requires a well-built physique, his male glamour looks are subtle and sophisticated. He brilliantly combines beautiful cut, fabrics with touch appeal and unbeatable colours. His suits show off the shoulders and cleverly indicate and shadow the body; he uses specially-made, exclusive fabrics, crêpe-handling wools, mixes of silk and wool, and silk and linen for the summer, all made in masculine versions of his 'Armani' colours – pale neutrals for summer and richer, deeper shades for autumn. Shirts are co-ordinated in complementary colours and patterns; raincoats and topcoats look classic but also elegantly modern, and he uses the finest suedes and leathers for his casualwear. Armani, like Chanel, has perfected the art of looking expensively dressed through quality rather than show.

America has never nurtured dictatorial couture designers in the same way as Europe; but Hollywood movie-star clothes and fashions that reflect the American way of life have been, and still are, an important international influence. Her best-known high-fashion designers are committed to producing clothes that are desirable and flattering, rather than trying to impose fashion directives and controversial silhouettes.

Calvin Klein has continued to offer his deceptively simple look of subtly-expensive, uncontrived chic; and Ralph Lauren, with his faultless classics, has been described as the designer who can dress people with 'new money' to look as if they were 'old money'. His style, perhaps more than any recent designer, depicts first and foremost an upper-class lifestyle; one that perhaps doesn't, and never did, actually exist in such a simplistic form – rather like the world portrayed in delightful old movies starring Katharine Hepburn and Cary Grant, or a dreamy nostalgic TV film set in some kind of time warp; an earlier period somewhere in between the 20s and the 50s.

Ralph Lauren's shops, especially the turn-of-the-cen-

Above: Power-dressing for men –
the sharp, *Wall-Street*-inspired
'yuppie' style.

Middle pic: Everyday jeans,
considered indispensable for
decades, went up-market in the
designer 80s.

Right and far right: Understated
Armani-style elegance – subtle
colours and masterly cut.

Left and above: As a reaction against the almost obsessional trend for basic black, bright, clear colours were promoted for day and evening clothes.

tury mansion on New York's Madison Avenue, convey a world of old-style elegance and understated glamour. His dressy womenswear is shown in drawing rooms, boudoirs and bedrooms of slightly faded grandeur. Sportswear is appropriately found down the hall in well-matured wardrobes and chests-of-drawers, and children's clothes are kept upstairs in suitably 'distressed' attic nurseries and playrooms.

Menswear is nonchalantly displayed in settings that resemble locker rooms in old established gentlemen's clubs, or grandfather's carefully-preserved dressing room; oars, tennis and squash rackets and riding crops together with a selection of well-worn riding, polo and hunting boots, are casually propped against walls, or slumped in corners as if abandoned by clean-cut young men as they rushed off to fight World War II.

Although Ralph Lauren's superb image-building promotion has undoubtedly helped to establish his style firmly in the public eye, his customers — male and female — have found his clothes relevant to their way of life. His womenswear — incorporating the uncluttered glamour of evening dresses and Dietrich-inspired dinner suits — good tailoring (simple and slow to date, or with the season's fashion themes, such as tartan or the nautical look) and his endlessly-useful sportswear, have all earned him devotees.

His top executive/landed gentry look for men has been equally successful. The English gentleman style of traditional, well-cut but not-too-sharp business suits, bespoke-looking shirts with the perfectly chosen tie, high-quality, conservative shoes and the Anglo-American alliance of navy blue blazers and tweed sports jackets, worn with striped shirts, jeans and loafers, have become popular in many countries. Lauren's clever marketing has also resulted in the considerable achievement of selling the British look — well-known for decades in London's St James's exclusive shops — back to the British.

Donna Karan, often considered the smart modern

The hairstyle of singer Annie Lennox and her penchant for wearing underwear as outerwear were widely copied.

woman's 'thinking designer', has very much in mind the busy lives of women who combine the demands of career, home, family and social life, and still want to look effortlessly well-dressed and glamorous. Her style is based on, and assembled around, the stretch body-suit, over which colour-toned garments are easily arranged. Topped with a beautifully-cut jacket, the body-suit looks like an expensive, carefully-co-ordinated sweater or T-shirt, and her sarong-style skirts can be smoothly draped on with the minimum of fuss and without the problems of underwear lines showing. A stunning example of Donna Karan's style was worn by Ivana Trump (ex-wife of American multi-million-aire Donald) when she was photographed for the January 1992 issue of American *Bazaar*: a long, pale grey tailored jacket with matching softly-draped, floaty skirt, worn over a silver stretch-tulle body-suit.

Away from the rarefied world of high fashion, American 'real life' clothes have become a major influence. The US sportswear style of inexpensive multi-coloured outfits – T-shirts and sweat-tops (with and without graphics), track-suits, brightly-printed shorts, stretch tops and shorts, ski caps and the inevitable Reebok trainers, functional and suited to the casual and pacey lifestyle – have become one of the most established ways of dressing in countries worldwide.

Recent reports about the emergence of the sharing, caring 'New Man' of the 90s – the man totally committed to equality between the sexes as well as a healthy lifestyle, wearing his unglamorous but easy-to-wash sweat top and pants, while he devotedly looks after the children – could be unrealistic and premature as far as the majority of men are concerned. Successfully-promoted male glamour images suggest that traditionally macho ideals are more popular and the fantasy image for many is still more likely to be Mel Gibson in *Mad Max* or even Arnold Schwarzenegger in *Terminator 2*, rather than the socially sensitive 'soft' man of the women's magazines.

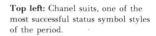

Top left: Chanel suits, one of the most successful status symbol styles of the period.

Bottom left: Dressy Ungaro designs were admired for their clever use of colours and prints.

Top right: Opulent-looking evening dresses with draped backs and flared hemlines.

Bottom right: The tailored jacket worn with a softly-draped skirt became an established fashion in the second half of the 80s.

Opposite: Karl Lagerfeld's 80s-update of a glamour classic – the sophisticated 'designer hat'.

Wearing heavy leather may not yet be mainstream fashion but the appeal of the 'biker' look has remained constant for nearly 40 years. It has become an unremarkable everyday way of dressing, and Marlon Brando, the original 'wild one' – glamorous leather-boy – is now a 67-year-old grandfather.

Male imagery of the present day is only slightly updated from ideals popularised in glamour's golden and pop ages. Kevin Costner's sex appeal, as with Valentino's in the 20s, and Errol Flynn's in the 30s, has been heightened by his dressing in dashing period costume for his starring roles in *Dances with Wolves*, and *Robin Hood, Prince of Thieves*.

Tom Cruise, in the highly-successful mid-80s film *Top Gun*, played an aggressive young American fighter pilot who fuelled his ego with his flying and womanising skills; a modern-day hero and an equivalent to the daring, brave, but less explicitly promiscuous pilots portrayed in so many films of the 40s. His *Top Gun* style – short military haircut, flying jacket, military fatigues, flat aviator boots, Rayban 'shades', flight badges and graphics – had a strong macho appeal, which remained a strong influence for several years.

The law enforcer and the detective, another standard Hollywood hero and anti-hero of the 40s and 50s and numerous TV films up to the present day, has also had an undeniable influence on men's fashions. Humphrey Bogart, in his fedora and belted trench coat, has become a classic Hollywood archetype, and Don Johnson's slightly dissipated chic in the popular TV series, *Miami Vice*, helped to promote designer-dressed policemen in the designer-obsessed 80s. His elegant, Italian-style, unstructured jackets with rolled-up sleeves, worn over pastel T-shirts, were teamed with baggy, pleated pants and slip-on shoes worn without socks. Most characteristic of all was Johnson's one-to-three-days' growth of beard, inevitably labelled 'designer stubble'. It was soon adopted by men in the design and media world, and

Opposite (top): As 'Maverick' in the 80s film *Top Gun*, Tom Cruise re-launched the glamorous fighter pilot look.

Above right: Hugo Boss promoted a combination of traditional and modern male glamour which appealed to men (and women!) everywhere.

Above: Don Johnson played the designer-dressed cop with 'designer stubble' in the hit TV series *Miami Vice*.

Opposite (bottom): George Michael replaced his earlier clean-cut appearance with darker, moodier looks and the obligatory 'designer stubble'.

then by men in other walks of life, in the questionable belief that it made them look more interesting and sexy.

Pop star George Michael *did* look good with his version of the unshaven look and he added more macho details to complete his own raunchy stage image: cropped hair showing off one earring, celebrity-style dark sunglasses, rugged (sometimes 'distressed') stone-washed jeans, heavily fringed leather jackets, and silver-tipped Western-style belts and cowboy boots.

Generally, pop stars have been less of a fashion influence. Even megastar Michael Jackson, with his specially-designed, glittering silver-and-black outfits, has been better known for the speculation about the apparent lightening of his skin colour and 'changing' facial features, rather than the style details of his clothes. Boy George's startling combination of Hassidic Jewish hat, long ethnic dreadlocks, asexual frock coats and tunics and immaculately-applied make-up, certainly formed an original concept which was mainly copied by other men in showbusiness, who became known as 'gender benders'. The gender-bender style received plenty of publicity but, unlike the idolised pop stars' looks and clothes of the 60s and 70s, it never became a widespread young fashion trend.

Glamour in men's fashions has remained surprisingly traditional throughout the 80s and into the 90s; today's slick businessman look – casually-elegant Italian designs, leather jackets, jeans and boots and 60s-inspired 'pop-age' styles – are all revised versions of classic 20th-century ways of dressing.

Change has concentrated more on improving men's looks and body development rather than radically new ideas in clothes. Grooming is considered very important with skilful individual hairstyling, sometimes dyed or high-lighted and moussed or gelled to give life and shine. Skincare is no longer thought unmanly and facials, skin toners and even discreet colouring are used by many men to help them look healthy and attractive.

The admired physique, which often requires consider-able effort to achieve through sport or physical training workouts, is the well-built athlete with broad shoulders, wide chest, slim but well-muscled torso and strong, well-developed thighs and calves. This is in stark contrast to the boyish, very slim figures so admired in the 60s, which now look far too thin and would be unsuitable for showing off today's masculine styles.

Individual fashion leaders, pop stars, film stars and celebrities, well-known for their unique personal style of hair, make-up and clothes, so memorable for their influence on clothes and looks in earlier decades, have – with a few exceptions – been less of a feature in recent years. Today's rich and famous tend to endorse rather than instigate fashion trends.

Some successful pop stars no longer seem to find it necessary to wear elaborately-contrived stage outfits to establish their image in the public's memory. Bruce Springsteen and Bryan Adams in their 'boy-next-door' basic T-shirts and jeans, have found enthusiastic audiences and worldwide fans quite happy to enjoy their personal cha-risma, music and special style of singing without the distraction of looking at them dressed in outrageous costumes.

Left: In the mid-80s, confronta-tional, controversial Madonna spawned millions of 'wanna-bees' worldwide.

Madonna, in complete contrast, has become famous for her heavily-promoted and often controversial imagery. In the early 80s, she was known for her 'homage-to-Marilyn-Monroe' look (Marilyn Monroe was her declared heroine and role model), and in the fun video for 'Material Girl', backed by a chorus of smartly-dressed adoring men, she looked delightfully early 50s, with her wavy blonde bob, defined make-up and strapless, pink silk ball dress. Her later styles sadly lost touch with the prettiness of her idol, and were much more blatantly provocative. She was one of the first to take advantage of the shock value of wearing lingerie and underwear in public. Dressed in exaggerated conical

Left and above: Ralph Lauren's 'Lifestyle' clothes – men's country-gentlemen casuals and the women's version of a 'Navaho Indian' jacket.

bras, suspenders and fishnet stockings, she went beyond the accepted norm for raunchy dressing, and her bizarre outfits with dangling suspenders worn over black tights looked more pre-Nazi Berlin than modern-day sex symbol.

The glamour 'renaissance', with its wide range of new and traditional options in looks and fashion, was a welcome development for older women. Many women reaching their 50s, who had enjoyed 30 years of exciting fashion changes, were not prepared to passively accept obvious signs of aging or settle for dull, older styles of dressing. There were more positive ways of minimising and combating age: flattering fashions, healthy eating, exercise programmes, and improved – albeit expensive – facial plastic surgery and body remodelling were there for the choosing.

Well-known women, including Joan Collins, Sophia Loren, Jane Fonda and Cher, increased their fame and were admired for their dedication to looking younger than their years, and for remaining sexy and attractive far beyond the previously-supposed time limit.

Clothes helped, particularly the revival of ideas from glamour's 'golden age'. Eighties interpretations of sophisticated hats with sweeping brims were shown off to greater advantage when worn by confident older women, as were sharply-tailored jackets with slight shoulder-padding (Margaret Thatcher's appearance improved and became more glamorous when she started to wear padded-shouldered suits and coats); Chanel suits; shorter but not-too-short straight skirts with dark, sheer tights and elegant, classic court shoes. Drapery, glitter-embroidered evening jackets, flowing evening dresses, all glamour classics, were guaranteed to flatter the figure- and fashion-conscious older woman.

Preserved good looks and figure, together with well-chosen clothes, were further enhanced by up-dated make-up and hairstyling. Professional advice on revising make-up, colouring and emphasis can be a great help to women who

have perhaps unwittingly stayed too long with the same cosmetics format and the ever-growing range of products has brought with it wonderful potential for improving and modernising looks. The deceptively casual but more arranged, fuller, shinier hairstyles introduced in the 80s were also a boon to mature women, and enabled them to wear longer, more flattering styles without looking as if they were trying to recapture their youth.

For centuries, Western European society has set fashion, with an American influence increasing during the last 70 years as the US recognised her lead in high standards of living and her position as the world's greatest 'Super Power'.

In more recent years, other powerful but still-emerging countries have so far tended to adopt and continue to follow Western styles, as an alternative to, or in preference to, their traditional way of dress. Japan's enormous economic strength and prosperity have made her one of the best markets for exporters of high-quality Western fashions, rather than other nations copying a strongly-stated traditional Japanese look.

Although some Japanese designers have proved to be extremely creative, with their 'cut-for-ease-of-movement' clothes, interesting, unrestrictive, flowing shapes, usually made in rather puritanical colours (a predominance of black, grey and black together, and stark white for contrasts or complete outfits), most of their designs have tended to mix traditional Japanese styling with established European concepts. A good example of this is Rei Kowakubo's highly successful designs for the stylish French-sounding Comme des Garçons shops.

Japanese designers caused a great deal of fashion interest in the early 80s; names such as Miyake, Rei Kowakubo, Yohji Kamamoto, and Kansi Yamamoto became internationally known. Their purer style was a refreshing contrast to the more dressed-up, showy looks gaining favour at the time. They were very much the designers' designers, appealing to fashion students and young followers of modern minimalist design. Their influence has been less far reaching than was expected, but their style, in a sense, is still on hold – possibly waiting to come into its own in the future, when simple, functional, less-aggressive clothes are more universally admired.

The increasing confidence of America's and Europe's expanding black population with their own made-up, fun, street styles has become a growing influence. Pulled around ski caps, bold graphics on T-shirts and sweats, big shirts worn outside pants, strong colours, brightly-patterned and skin-tight fluorescent stretch shorts, baggy 'rap' trousers, and ankle-covering, loosely-laced trainers have all been absorbed into the international teenage fashion scene. Successful white pop artists, like New Kids on the Block and Vanilla Ice, helped to make their own images universally popular by adopting the cool black style; even some of the upper-class young British, once so conservative and convention-ally dressed, have enjoyed wearing their out-of-school 'rap' fashions.

Fashion has come a long way in the last ten years or so. In the first half of the period, unabashed elitist dressing reflected the growing gulf between the haves and have-nots inside individual countries and throughout the world; well-fed, well-developed bodies in strongly-stated establishment 'rich people' fashions made the rift more apparent than at any time since the Second World War.

Women's silhouettes – built-out shoulders accentuating shaped bodices and waists, hips highlighted with peplums and drapery, conservative skirt lengths and elegant shoes – the big-man look of menswear, wide-shouldered suits and the more categorised range of status-symbol dressing – all characterised an age when acquiring wealth and showing, if not flaunting it, was such an admired ideal.

The turbulent historic events of the late 80s and early 90s, growing instability, the break up of the USSR and her East European empire, booms, crashes and world recession have been well-mirrored by a kind of fashion anarchy.

Power-dressing, like so many other symbols of author-ity, has been deposed, but the romantic appeal of glamour's 'golden age' of the great couturiers, and the gods and the goddesses of the Silver Screen has continued. The fun and vitality of the carefree 'pop age', futuristic fashions, leather gear and boots, fantasy dressing, hippie looks, glam rock and even the return of punk are being enjoyed again. The high-fashion ideal is younger than it has been for 20 years, with considerable emphasis on body- and leg-show.

Provocative body-show is widely promoted for the totally liberated young woman of the 90s. The daring of wearing lingerie as daytime outerwear – ever skimpier garments decorated with more and more glitter, patterning and embellishment – and the current trend for lycra stretch tops, bathing-suit dresses, micro-length skirts, shorts and body-suits, are all part of the new frankness in fashion.

Trends are numerous and often contradictory, and in complete and refreshing contrast to all the 'do you think I'm sexy?' looks, the cool, classic, unpretentious and more subtle, feminine styles of Grace Kelly and Audrey Hepburn in the 50s are also being revived. The functional ease of wearing active-sportswear-type garments for pressurised everyday life is also a firmly established concept.

Past, present and forward-looking fashions are available and can be mixed together in a way unimaginable in earlier decades. Rather like computer data, fashion information is a modern resource; the range of 'looks' and 'lines' for both sexes have never been more diverse. The preoccupation with attaining, through natural or artificial means, the currently-admired facial looks and body shape grows ever more popular.

After 60 years of continual change and revision, the scope for interpreting glamour in fashion has never been more extensive.

Today, in the less comfortable, 'never had it so bad' atmosphere of the early 90s, the whole relevance of fashion in its present form is being questioned. The expense, hype and extravagance of high fashion are all being

Glamour Today

unflatteringly spotlighted: staggering fees for top model girls, a single Paris couture dress costing the price of an average home in an affluent country, and the exaggerated importance given to yet another revision in the placing of necklines and hemlines all seem

Opposite: 'Supermodel' Cindy Crawford showing the enduring appeal of classic glamour looks – the soft bob and the lacy bustier top.

far removed from the 'real world' to many people, and the once-revered designer collections are viewed far more critically.

The recently aspired-to ideal of 'designer clothes, is often subject to almost immoral connotations for being too closely associated with the discredited, acquisitive character of the 80s, whose attitudes and policies are blamed for many of today's problems.

Traumatic social upheavals always result, not only in major changes in the way people dress, but also in complete alterations in what constitutes 'fashion'.

The shock of the French Revolution swept away the blatant over-show of wealth, rank and privilege; women's towering pompadour powdered wigs, encrusted bodices and huge panniered skirts, and men's almost as elaborate wigs, brocade jackets, ornate waistcoats, knee breeches and silk stockings, were all quickly replaced by far less conspicuous ways of dressing. Women adopted classic Grecian curls and simple high-waisted 'Directoire' shift dresses; while men wore the English country gentleman style of unadorned cutaway coats, plain waistcoats and long breeches tucked into high boots.

The destabilising effects of the First World War gave the final push to the post-Victorian age with its elaborately covered-up, figure-constraining clothes, and the jazzy fashions of the 20s took over. Women cut their hair, painted their faces and shortened their skirts to knee-length. Men enjoyed wearing easier-fitting, less strictly-formal clothes.

The changes following the even more destructive Second World War were slightly delayed to allow for basic recovery, and the acceptance of the Cold War status quo. When they arrived – in the 'Swinging 60s' – they were just as radical: flowing manes, space-age and hippie styles, unisex and asexual dressing. Anything 'went' as long as it was youth-orientated and experimental.

The present social and national upheavals – recession, concern for the environment, and the limitless possibilities for automation and technology – are bound to be reflected in more far-reaching changes in the interpretation of fashion. There are already indications about the form these changes may take and the wider scope and character of glamour in fashion at the turn of *this* century, and possibly into the early decades of the 21st century, is beginning to emerge.

The rich source of past fashions (particularly the well-recorded recent past, endlessly promoted by media coverage), films and TV programmes continually acclaim retro influences, and constant fashion revivals have made people so familiar with the styles of the past that they are seen more and more as fashion options of the present. In the future, some people may choose to dress from head-to-toe in the designs of their favourite era, as an occasional or important feature of their own individual style. There is a growing market for interesting retro clothes; apart from being comparatively inexpensive, they are admired for their cut, quality of fabrics, period charm, and the 'personal statement' interest they give the wearer.

Admired ideals of glamour in fashion during the last 65 years, already widely used, have plenty to offer the style-conscious. Periods and designs can be interchanged at will: the dressy with the casual, the high-class with the streetwise

Above: Karl Lagerfeld's stunning black-and-white embroidered outfit for Chanel.

Left: Top model Naomi Campbell 'wigged out' in silver, wearing Thierry Mugler's futuristic show-girl look.

and film-star looks; the permutations are endless and each 'glamour age' has something to contribute.

Glamour's 'golden age' has given us many classic looks and unbeatable formats for dressing with style. Examples from its rich heritage include:

The hairstyles of the famous screen goddesses, particularly the flattering long bob falling over one eye and turned under on the shoulders, originally worn by Garbo, Ginger Rogers, Rita Hayworth, and Veronica Lake who was especially well known for her extra long version, and the sophisticated alternative – upswept hair, arranged on top of the head in neo-Edwardian waves and curls. Both have become hairstyle classics, copied by countless women. Men have always loved the femininity of long, loose hair, and the letting down of hair, like the rolling down of stockings, has been described as an erotic symbol of a woman lowering her defences!

Glamorous hats with sweeping brims can give women an air of class, presence and occasion, and chic pillboxes, draped in veiling, offer a wonderfully sophisticated, pampered look.

Coco Chanel's expensive understatement is as effective as ever – the impractical luxury of all-white, creamy beige or pearl-grey outfits in supple fabrics – pure linen, silk jersey, crêpe and crêpe-de-chine – and uncontrived evening wear, a glittering cardigan-jacket over a chiffon slip, or a simple satin or velvet sheath, dressed up with stunning jewellery. All these proven successes still have an undeniable influence on designers like Giorgio Armani, Donna Karan, Calvin Klein and Ralph Lauren.

Sharp tailoring with square shoulders, introduced by Schiaparelli in the 30s and worn so effectively by Joan Crawford, the original 'power dresser', have helped to give women a presence and a confident, cosmopolitan 'I know my way around' look. Shouldery suits became an essential feature of the 1980s smart female executive and have only slowly lost favour in the 90s.

The sophisticated sex appeal of two contrasting female images, first popularised 60 years ago, remains as strong as ever. Body-curves outlined in long, clinging underslip-dresses with halter-necklines and low backs, and the intriguing covering up of glamorous women in men's clothes (Marlene Dietrich and Katharine Hepburn) continue in juxtaposition. Among the masculine styles popular with women are baggy white yachting pants worn with loose sweaters and blazers, tailored trouser-suits and, most effective of all, black silk-revered dinner suits with matching black pants (as recently worn by the Princess of Wales).

The timeless beauty of expertly-draped dresses, inspired by Ancient Greece and Rome, has never lost its appeal; perfected by Madame Gres before the Second World War, they are bound to be admired by future generations.

Christian Dior brought back the hourglass figure which had been such a major feature of fashion in earlier centuries. His strapless bustier-topped dresses, nipped-in waists and long, tight, slit skirts, or full bouffant skirts, dazzled post-World War II women. His silhouettes looked supremely elegant on the fashion models of the time and delightfully sexy and curvy on young film stars like Elizabeth Taylor and Marilyn Monroe. Accentuating the figure returned again in the 80s and it is such an hereditary instinct that it is sure to have many more revivals.

Sheer stockings and elegant, high-heeled court shoes and strappy high-heeled sandals, so sensational when they were first shown in public in the 20s, are all-time favourites and – like so many of 'glamour's golden age' looks for women – too sexy to be out of vogue for long.

Men's glamour looks from the same era are less memorable but some have become admired classics. These include the officer in immaculate dress uniform (used so effectively by Hollywood and Nazi Germany); the groomed 'pretty boy' good looks and sleek, short hair of the early film stars, which have already been revived in a less precious form; and the internationally-aspired-to imagery of the perfectly-turned-out gentleman. The 'ideal', although not always considered fashionable, has remained surprisingly unchanged over the decades. Stylish men still dress for town in elegant bespoke suits, shirts and shoes, and off duty in Ralph Lauren-style country-house settings, continue to wear blazers and flannels or tweed jackets, Scottish knitwear and cords and – for elitist shows of glamour – hunting- and polo-gear with riding breeches and polished riding boots (all guaranteed to convey a masculine world of good breeding, proficiency, wealth and power).

Pop-age glamour has provided a very different store of younger, less formal fashion options: extrovert styles, for both sexes, with practical appeal as well as fun and fantasy images.

Glamour in young men's fashion became a much more important feature and early pop-age heroes – James Dean, Marlon Brando and Elvis Presley – with their 'moody' good looks and biker/Western styles of dress, have never lost their cool, anti-establishment appeal, and are even more romanticised and commercialised rôle models today than when they first became famous over thirty years ago.

Brigitte Bardot's backcombed, loosely-arranged 'bee-hive' hairdos, with or without cascading side-curls, loved in the 60s, hated in the 70s, and successfully revived in the 80s, have become accepted standard styles of the 90s. Similarly, long, loose hairstyles for men, so characteristic of the late 60s and early 70s, then out of fashion until a few years ago, are seen today as alternative mainstream styles.

Mini-length hemlines, once the only correct skirt length, re-established in the last decade (after several attempts), have now become an unremarkable basic length which, like other standard hemlines, will probably wax and wane in popularity with fashion's ever-changing moods.

Clothes and boots in leather or shiny, simulated leather effects, thought so daringly 'kinky' when they were first introduced in the early 60s, have become an established part of fashion. Although extremely popular, single leather garments are generally worn as part of outfits rather than as a whole. The raunchy full leather-gear of the catwalks – Gianni Versace's glitter-embroidered 'Rockers' and Thierry Mugler's futuristic, thigh-booted 'Space-Age Masters' (furtively admired, or considered too strongly stated and jokey), may come into their own in the future, when remaining inhibitions about 'appropriate' dressing have been shed.

Bright, strong colours and pop-age prints, hot-coloured abstracts and optical effects (black and white 'op art'), popularised in the 60s, have been even more successful in the late 80s and early 90s, particularly boldly-printed tights and more colourful menswear. Women in mini-tunics over fancy-patterned tights and men in brightly-coloured jackets, strongly-printed tops and shorts – all easy-to-wear, young, forward-looking fashions – seem set to remain modern basics for many years to come.

Ethnic influences from Asian countries, North American Indians and Latin America first became a significant trend a generation ago as 'cult' styles (the hippie look), or alternative, fun ways of dressing. Recently, Japanese 'purist' styling has offered another interesting option. 'Other cultures' interpretation of fashion will inevitably become more important as the world grows smaller with more integration between nations.

Jeans must be the most international garment in the history of fashion. Worn throughout the world by rich and poor and old and young alike, as a part of high fashion, to show off the figure or for functional workwear, they were originally introduced in 19th-century North America as gold-prospectors' work pants. Quickly adopted by cowboys and farmers, they were successfully commercialised by Levi Strauss and are now referred to simply as 'Levi's'. The wearing of jeans steadily increased from the 1940s onwards

Above: The 'dangerously handsome' looks of movie stars like Matt Dillon helped to revive rogue-ish glamour for men.

Right: Jason Priestly, teen idol and star of the hit TV series *Beverly Hills 90210*, has re-created the 'glamorous rebel' look.

The quiet glamour of *Pretty Woman* star, Julia Roberts, has made her world famous.

but they really became a 'way of life' garment in the 'pop age'. Their popularity may lessen occasionally but they are the best example to date of an always-present style that never seems to lose its appeal with each successive generation.

Although indulgent revivals of 'pop-age' styling have been widely promoted and enjoyed in the last few years, many of its basic concepts have, in fact, never been out of fashion. Jeans and T-shirts, colourful casual-wear, ethnic influences, fashion boots, leather, and glamorous pop-star looks for men – with varied degrees of emphasis and revision – have all become an established part of contemporary dressing.

Fashion's most recent glamour update, going forward in the 90s, has already added new concepts and ideas to the developing range of fashion choices. Recurring and persistent themes have included leading designers' almost Byzantine love of patternings, rich colours, embroideries and jewel-like embellishments for dressy day outfits as well as evening-wear. All represent the revival of impressive, almost gaudy, showiness in dress, more reminiscent of earlier centuries than the familiar dress conventions of the 20th century.

Daring, skimpy, body-revealing fashions always characterise periods of great social change; our unstable times are no exception and are reflected in designers' preoccupation with putting women into sexy lingerie for everyday wear. Pretty, low-cut, lacy bras, silky and see-through slips, 30s-style satin- or lace-trimmed cami-knickers, long and short panties and fishnet stockings with suspenders are all considered unconventional when displayed in public. However, the underwear influence on day dressing *is* growing.

The perfected body shape and the elitist superiority of the proficient sportsman and woman is one of today's most popular ideals. Wearing stretch garments that are comfortable, functional and draw attention to the entire body form is an assured mass-appeal style for the present era and will probably last well into the next century.

Fashion resources of the past and present are accumulating to provide a wonderfully varied source of influences and inspirations. But what are the new ideas and developments that are going to enlarge and define 'glamour in fashion' in the immediate future?

Present-day gurus of style and looks offer more advice than ever before on how to acquire film-star and fashion-magazine glamour. It involves a basic dedication to self-improvement which requires considerable hard work and expense for most people. The whole process is more than skin deep and starts with perfecting the body both inside and out – a balanced diet for health, looks and performance is considered essential.

Magazines and newspapers continually offer revelations about the 'best', the 'most effective' and 'correct' diets, and the virtuous self-denial of going on a diet is presented as an admired, modern-day, puritanical quality. Apart from helping a person to achieve a fashionable shape, correct eating is promoted as vital for improving and maintaining good health. Although undoubtedly true in specific cases, medical opinion on the benefits of following popular regulated diets is divided, and definite links between illness and undisciplined eating have yet to be confirmed.

Along with dieting, techniques for relaxation and posture can also help in the quest for a glamorous body. In the US, modern centres, which are off-shoots of the long-established aims of health farms, concentrate on two age-old body aids – fasting and yoga. 'Counselled fasting' is reported to detoxify the body, improve skin quality and clarify the mind so that it can be more receptive to the relaxing benefits of yoga.

The 'Alexander Technique', which originated in the early part of the century, became more generally well known in recent decades, and today there are a growing number of teachers and pupils worldwide. The Technique can undoubtedly have the pleasing benefits of making those who practise

Opposite: The high-priority of the 90s – the worked on, toned physique in body-moulding lycra.

it look and feel better. It aims to re-educate and improve posture, which tends to deteriorate from young adulthood onwards. Apart from helping spinal problems, enhancing general well-being and encouraging the ability to relax, correct posture can dramatically improve the look of the body with increased height, better head and neck carriage, broadened shoulders, a lengthened torso and an adjusted and improved balance to the pelvis, which in turn helps the legs to be more supple.

Diet and posture adjustments can be combined with workout exercise programmes to get the body into the admired shape of the 90s. There is an ever-growing range of exercise books and videos for those who want to follow a programme at home. Adverts for such material proclaim, 'For a perfect behind spend 20 minutes on your bottom', and go on to explain, 'A perfect bottom, a flat stomach, a pair of lissom legs. Whatever your heart desires, your body can start to achieve in just 20 minutes a day.' Three separate videos are recommended, each one compiled to get the specified area into shape.

For people who prefer – or feel they need – the discipline of working under supervision, gym classes and the use of the gym are well established, and the individual attention of the 'personal trainer' has become extremely popular.

Personal trainers compile 'lifestyle' regimes of exercises and involvement in some active sport to suit the age, fitness level and body objectives of each client, and sometimes offer dietary advice as part of their keep-fit and body-development programmes. The obvious advantages of such attention undoubtedly appeal to serious body-developers, especially the not-so-young who may understandably feel shy or intimidated by the prospect of 'working out' in groups, where they may compare unfavourably with energetic, 'in-shape' younger men and women.

Personal trainers' status and fees can vary considerably and range from young PE instructors charging a modest amount on an ad hoc basis for working in their spare time in clients' homes or at a communal gym, to high-profile Californian-style 'trainers to the stars', who instruct in their own impressively well-equipped gyms, or visit at the offices or home gyms of their clients. Their services are very much in demand and can be expensive – they usually require contracts (including an 'on-screen credit' clause for the films of their star pupils) and often expect their potential clients to be recommended to them!

Although superbly-defined muscles, like those of the famous American showboys, The Chippendales, are an unrealistic ideal for most men, well-developed bodies for both sexes have never been a more important part of glamour in fashion, and look like becoming even more essential with the on-going trends in body-conscious clothes. It is no longer enough to be slim. In fact, the ultra-slim model girl image, which has been declining in popularity for the last decade, is no longer admired, and the well-known view, attributed to the late, always chic, Duchess of Windsor that, 'a woman can never be too thin or too rich', certainly doesn't apply to the fashion ideals of today – as far as the first part is concerned, at least!

Plastic surgery, which has been available for decades, is now often seen as an important aid in achieving fashionable, glamorous looks, and is considered very newsworthy. The traditional reasons for wanting to undergo cosmetic surgery – unattractive or misshapen features and signs of aging – are as relevant as ever but there are, however, also a growing number of good-looking young people (mainly women) who want to change their looks and figure to suit the popular fashion ideals. In the refined 50s, the little turned-up nose was the 'chic' nose-job fashion models and society women wanted. More recently, with the fashion for bolder, sexier looks and bodies, fuller lips and larger breasts have been at the top of many women's shopping lists. Bad publicity over breast implants has caused a temporary tailing off in the demand for that particular operation, but the general scope for changing looks and body shape is growing all the time.

Removing unwanted fat (by lipo-suction) has considerable appeal for those who have battled in vain with diets and exercises for years It can be particularly successful for reducing fat in specific areas such as the hips and thighs, but is obviously less effective for the overall obese body. The frightening fantasy scenario portrayed in the black comedy film, *She-Devil* (based on Fay Weldon's book *Life and Loves of a She-Devil*), where it was possible to be remodelled as an exact replica of someone else in the physical sense, may be a long way off, but the range of plastic surgery and relating operations are bound to become ever more extensive in the future.

Leading plastic surgeons, Bryan Mayou and Barry Jones, who are familiar with the latest developments which have only been touched on in this section, point out that any kind of plastic surgery needs to be carefully considered by anyone planning to undergo it in any form. They also reiterate the well-publicised dangers of over-sunning. It *does* cause premature aging of the skin and protection from harmful ultra-violet rays should start from babyhood onwards.

Fashion magazines no longer promote deep tans. In fact, they have not been 'fashion magazine fashionable' for some time, and many of today's Californian sex symbols don't sunbathe at all. For some people who live in sunny climates, it has become a form of inverted snobbery to be deliberately pale, unlike the attitudes of many from the northern hemisphere who, deprived of the sun for much of the year, like to return from their vacation in a hotter climate with a deep 'had a good time' suntan.

Attitudes towards sunbathing have turned full circle in the last 65 years. Until the late 20s, people took the sun in small doses – they didn't want to look what they thought of as 'peasant brown', and hoped to return from their holidays looking relaxed and fit with a good healthy colour. Today's aspirations are exactly the same.

Dauntingly high standards of facial beauty and figure development (worked-at natural assets, or artificially aided), have already become the most aspired-to basis for glamorous looks.

Although not as extensively or as obsessively as today, generations of men have gone in for 'body-building'; women's involvement started later, and serious 'working out', parallel to men's, is comparatively recent. Women's dedication to getting in shape is very different from the attitudes of earlier periods when corsetry contrived and contorted their figures into exaggerated curves to heighten their sex appeal. As recently as the 50s, boned bras and 'waspies' helped to produce the fashionable 'all woman' shape, and the traditional titillation of giving the boys 'an eyeful' was still the main motivation.

In the more liberated 90s, the attitudes of both sexes have become much more similar. Naturally, men and women want their bodies to be admired and desired, but the celebration of a perfected body as a symbol of health, strength and superiority and for pure self-esteem – instinctive in men since earliest times – is now becoming equally important to women. The 'Wonderwoman' as well as the 'Superman' ideal, long predicted in books, films and on TV, is fast becoming a reality.

Hairstyling and make-up are extending the scope of what constitutes fashion. Until this decade, although sometimes subject to retro influences, both had a recognisable look of the time, and many women tended to stay longer with their style of make-up and hair than with their selection of changing and alternative fashions in clothes. In the 90s, however, the range of options is much wider: 30s, 40s, 50s and 60s styles, unadulterated or combined with present-day ideas, together with some new concepts, are all on offer.

Characterised 'period' make-up – deep red, 30s Jean Harlow mouths, Lana Turner's defined eyes and lips on smooth foundation colour from the 40s, Audrey Hepburn's emphasised eyebrows, and Brigitte Bardot's false eyelashes and pearly-pink, pouting lips of the 60s – are all equally fashionable looks for the retro purist. In slightly softer, up-dated forms they hold a more general appeal.

Styling has become much more individual and leading make-up artists and hairdressers continually emphasise the importance of and their dedication to customised looks. Today, a woman can concentrate on the deceptively simple objective of enhancing her natural looks with all the subtle make-up aids that are available, and can complement her 'look' with a soft, flattering, uncontroversial hairstyle. Alternatively, a more design-orientated woman can choose a defined fashion style. A glamour's 'golden age' mixture of 40s and early-50s styles is an easy to wear option – side-parted hair, finger-waved to fall forward, and gently curled onto the shoulders, framing an evenly made-up face with glamorously emphasised eyes and lips.

To complete the lure of the 'lingerie look' in clothes, seductive hairstyling and make-up are a must. Hair is carefully arranged to give a slightly dishevelled look; loosely-set curls are partly swept up and partly allowed to cascade down. Smoothly made-up faces, lightly powdered, are given 'movie star' eyes with arched eyebrows, pearly eye-shadow, false eyelashes, and liquid eyeliner drawn on to slightly elongate the lids. Achieving the much-admired, soft, sexy mouth is helped by exaggerating the size of the lips, with the outer edges shaded in a dark colour and a lighter tone used towards the centre. Rose shades are popular and, to give further subtle emphasis, lip balm is applied and finely dusted with powder.

Wilder, more theatrical looks, especially those for hair,

Left: Seen at an awards ceremony with fellow megastar Michael Jackson, Madonna revels in her Monroe-inspired look.

Above: Natural brunette Madonna in the evening/underwear look she made so popular – jewelled bodysuit and black stockings.

are influenced by the 60s and feature really 'big' hairdos, curled, teased and lifted to produce lustrous, 'sure to be noticed' leonine manes. Hairpieces are sometimes added to give even more volume and, for the really avant-garde, styles are compiled with intentionally obvious false hair: 'wigged-out', oversized chignons, corkscrew curls and styles made up with startling chunks of colour. Black-and-red striped fringes over neat blonde bobs, or long, shoulder-touching golden blonde 'flick-ups' topped by a dark brown fringe, highlighted with silver streaks, are not uncommon. All teamed with heavy make-up (emphasised eyebrows, thickly-lashed, outlined eyes, and strongly-stated, richly-coloured mouths), the look is obviously contrived.

Top model girls excel in showing off the impact of directional fashion 'statements'. Megastars such as Claudia Schiffer, Linda Evangelista, Naomi Campbell and Cindy Crawford, although admired and famous for their stunning personal looks, are also extremely successful because they can be so effectively transformed – with the aid of make-up, hair and pose – into the individual leading designers' fashion images of the season. Their professionalism has made them like actresses in that their looks can be altered to suit the role they are portraying, without losing their own identity. Showbusiness and modelling have become increasingly similar; models look like movie stars and many well-known actresses, including Julia Roberts and Kim Basinger,

The 'Supermodels': In the early 90s, Linda Evangelista went from brunette to blonde to redhead – a fashion metamorphosis.

Cindy Crawford in a 30s-inspired hip-clinging dress.

are former models. Both professions enjoy the same kind of status, publicity and acclaim.

Present-day women are much more aware of the rapidly expanding choice of hairstyles and make-up. Newspapers and magazines devote more space than ever before to well-informed advice on hair and beauty, and illustrate the importance of co-ordinating them with fashionable themes in clothes, giving importance to the 'top-to-toe' look.

In the future, women are likely to enjoy the fun and impact of showing greater variations in their own overall style presentation. The design interest of the clothes may sometimes be predominant, or alternatively, hair and make-up may be the focal point, supported by simple, underplayed,

Claudia Schiffer in a 90s version of the 'little black dress'.

complementary clothes. Fashion's widening horizons certainly present an exciting prospect, particularly for the ultra style-conscious. But with ever more choice and fewer fashion conventions, will the average woman and man be able to cope? Or will the number of fashion 'victims' increase dramatically? And are we going to see a growing need for fashion therapy and counselling?

The developing trends and the feeling of anticipation that are recharging glamour in fashion for women are less evident for men. Some developments, such as non-aggressive, softer-shouldered silhouettes in cool, powdery pastels and elegant neutral shades, or more extrovert, strong, clear colours and active sportswear influences, do co-relate. The leading fashion looks, however, are far less unisex than they were during the 60s and early 70s.

The uninhibited use of embellishment – embroideries, jewel-like decorations and multi-patterning – so popular for women, have so far mainly been reserved for male pop stars' outfits; and a bedroom look for men (apart from 'designer stubble') has, so far (thankfully?), not been launched as an important fashion trend for men.

More traditional menswear – the business and professional man's suit (so unchanged throughout the century that future fashion historians may find it difficult to date it to any specific decade) – has, in fact, in its younger man's fashion form, been subject to minor, but regular, revisions. After the over-sharp, over-slick, Wall Street 'yuppie' style of the 80s, the 90s fashion suits are suitably contrite. Teamed with tie-less shirts, they have sloped shoulders, narrower-fitting, buttoned-up jackets and loosely-cut trousers without pressed creases.

The division between formal, casual and sports wear is less defined. A smart silky suit can be worn with a simple cotton T-shirt and black Chelsea boots; an immaculately-tailored wool jacket over a Levi's denim jacket and a striped T-shirt, worn outside basic jeans; a linen suit and waistcoat without a shirt underneath, and a formal, calf-length overcoat over a denim shirt, jeans and biker boots – all apparently random mixes, they are, in fact, current looks for men.

Male role model ideals are not as widely varied or as dramatic as women's, but they are becoming less stereotyped and more multi-racial. The keen young sportsman/business executive with a fresh face and well-cut, blond highlighted hair of a few years ago is less popular today. More 'interesting' male images are in fashion, particularly dark, moody, Hispanic and mixed-race looks. The 'ideal' is taller and tougher-looking – just as style-conscious as his 80s counterpart but in a less classical and conformist way. Greased-back 30s gigolo hairstyles, cropped, updated GI crewcuts, carefully-arranged rocker quiffs and sideboards, waxed ethnic curls and dreadlocks and 'pop-age', shoulder-length manes are all equally fashionable, and open to personal interpretation.

For creating an aura of hero-worshipped glamour, goodlooking sportsmen are on an equal level to most stylish movie stars. This has never been more evident than it is today with successful sports personalities involved in lucrative deals to endorse various products and fashion lines.

Handsome soccer stars, like Britain's Gary Lineker and John Barnes, are often photographed in expensive designer clothes, and established cricket greats, such as Ian Botham and Imran Khan, have also been promoted for their interest in fashion, making them popular role models for men and pin-ups for hordes of women. Famous tennis players and boxers also have many admirers, and the muscled physique of the British middleweight champion, Gary Stretch, and the exotic looks and impressive body of tennis ace Yannick Noah, got them voted onto the list of Europe's 50 sexiest men of 1990.

The elegant glamour of the equestrian sports never loses its appeal. The classical style of formal riding clothes

Opposite (top): World-class British athlete Steve Backley was among many promoting stylishness in sport.

In the 90s, the glamorous couple seemed to be everywhere . . .

Opposite: Simon and Yasmin le Bon.

Left: Kim Basinger and Alec Baldwin.

Above: David Bowie and Iman.

The classy yachting look – Ralph Laurens' beautifully cut jacket and pants.

Fashion looks of 1992 – the newly important long, slit skirt (right) and the masculine but elegant trouser suit (left).

for showjumping, dressage and hunting originated in 18th-century England and has evolved over the generations. Most of the original concept has remained and today, men and women continue the tradition of wearing black riding hats (now reinforced for extra protection), elegant stock at the neck, perfectly-tailored riding jackets in black or red (i.e. hunting pink) with black velvet half-collars, white or creamy beige riding breeches (usually in stretch twill), and highly-polished black-or mahogany-topped black leather riding boots.

English riding clothes are still admired all over the world and, for those who can afford them, hats from Lock's, and boots from Lobb's of St James's, together with jackets and breeches from Huntsmen of Saville Row, are still the ultimate in style, quality and 'snob' appeal.

Skill in equestrian sports and the glamour of the clothes undoubtedly boost egos and enhance images. Princess Michael of Kent looks wonderfully elegant and feminine in her formal riding clothes, and Prince Charles's sex appeal on the polo field has been mentioned many times. He may have been startled to read in the February, 1992, issue of society magazine *Tatler*, an in-depth article on the potency of his

Extrovert high fashion – the dazzling use of colour, patterning and embellishment.

Ungaro's ruched, body-conscious glamour dress.

polo appeal, posing the question 'Is Prince Charles Too Sexy for His Own Good?'

The glamour of polo has been appreciated by Hollywood since its earliest days; it was and still is brought into many movies to help create a high society atmosphere. Hollywood greats, such as Spencer Tracy, enjoyed the game as one of their favourite sports, and the tradition is carried on by some of today's famous stars, including Stefanie Powers and Sylvester Stallone.

In today's tough, unstable times, the influence of dashing yet functional sportswear on everyday clothes is as

Glittery glamour from Chanel.

popular as ever. The riding look, whether classic English or cowboy Western, is a recurring fashion theme. The glamour of ski-wear, so impressively illustrated in the 1992 Winter Olympics — brilliant colours, all-silver outfits, exciting prints and futuristic-looking ski helmets — are bound to boost the established influence of ski clothes. Parkas, anoraks, ski jackets and ski-style pants are already commercially-successful, mass-market fashions, as are many other unisex sports garments.

Recently-interviewed fashion students at the Royal College of Art in London, the trendsetting designers of the

Chanel in the 90s — slick and sexy in indigo-toned stretch tweed.

future, have surprisingly down-to-earth attitudes to glamour – perhaps because of the recessionary times. They visibly shudder at the memory of the greedy 80s, particularly *Dallas*- and *Dynasty*-style 'glamour'. In addition, some of the best-known, long-established Paris couturiers are considered out of touch by most of the students, still using shapes and fashion ideas from the last decade.

Many of the students value the cut, quality and classicism of Armani clothes and also like the fun appeal of Jean Paul Gaultier's designs. Opinion on showy designers, like Christian Lacroix, Gianni Versace and Karl Lagerfeld, is divided, and there is a general feeling that the obvious consideration of the variety of women's looks, sizes and shapes is missed by some designers, who are all too anxious to promote their strong fashion 'statements' and uncompromising but limited 'images'. Several students mentioned the need for a centre path in fashion, more creative and interesting than the very simple and classic, but purer than the recent trends for the overuse of glitter, loud prints and bold, clashing colours, all of which women soon tire of, it was felt.

In today's world, the cost of high fashion was considered truly shocking and difficult to justify from the sellers' or the buyers' point of view. Some students felt so strongly about this that they went as far as describing it as 'obscene'.

Like all recent generations, they have grown up with an affection for retro looks. They respect the stylishness of the 30s and 40s, and adore the 50s – particularly the Hollywood kitsch of the period – but feel that the 60s and 70s have already been overplayed and over-commercialised.

The subtle appeal of gentlemanly elegance as represented by movie stars, particularly Cary Grant, was mentioned several times, but the sharp-shouldered suits of the recent past were considered almost as tasteless as *Dynasty* looks for women.

It was generally felt that men should care and be keenly interested in their appearance but that it was unmanly to do so too obviously. The students felt that cleverly-chosen, deceptively-casual separates are the most appropriate way of dressing for most men of today.

Models' appearances and styles are seen as an important influence on young women's looks, as well as on those of the rich and famous, and Madonna receives credit and respect for challenging the 'norm' and trying out a variety of controversial fashions.

So much for the views of future designers and the many other influences affecting fashions and looks; the question is, where is fashion heading next?

Glamour in fashion today is all about variety and choice. Money certainly helps to achieve selective ideals, but stylishness is not necessarily about displaying wealth. Dictatorial designers, together with mega pop and movie stars, so dominant in the past, no longer have as much power or authority. Inflated egos are much more vulnerable to the all-seeing, critical eyes of the media and can be quickly deflated and debunked.

Increasing freedom of style is likely to characterise fashion in the immediate future, and Cole Porter's 'Anything Goes' comment on society and fashion in the 20s, could become 'Anarchy Goes' in the years leading up to the end of the 20th century.

Looking at the possibilities further ahead, one thing is certain: fashion, as always, will reflect the times. If through choice or necessity, the world has to accept a much simpler way of life, many of the style attitudes of the 1990s will become irrelevant and impossible to achieve. Should a more controlled and conformist society be established, its aims and aspirations will inevitably be mirrored in its clothes. In complete contrast, if the long-predicted world of super-advanced technology becomes a reality, with almost unlimited scope for comfort and leisure, fashion will lose the practical restrictions that have kept it in check for most of

Armani's perfected minimalism —
unadorned, collarless jacket and
brief skirt.

Katharine Hamnett's raunchy glamour look for men and women set the catwalk on fire.

the 20th century. Extreme, totally impractical styles, unlike anything known since before the French Revolution, could return — at least for the favoured elite.

Whatever the future holds, fashion will adapt. There will be many more interpretations of that intriguing extra quality, the sparkle in admired clothes and looks that is glamour in fashion.

Index